HOW TO DRAW
FOR
MINECRAFTERS

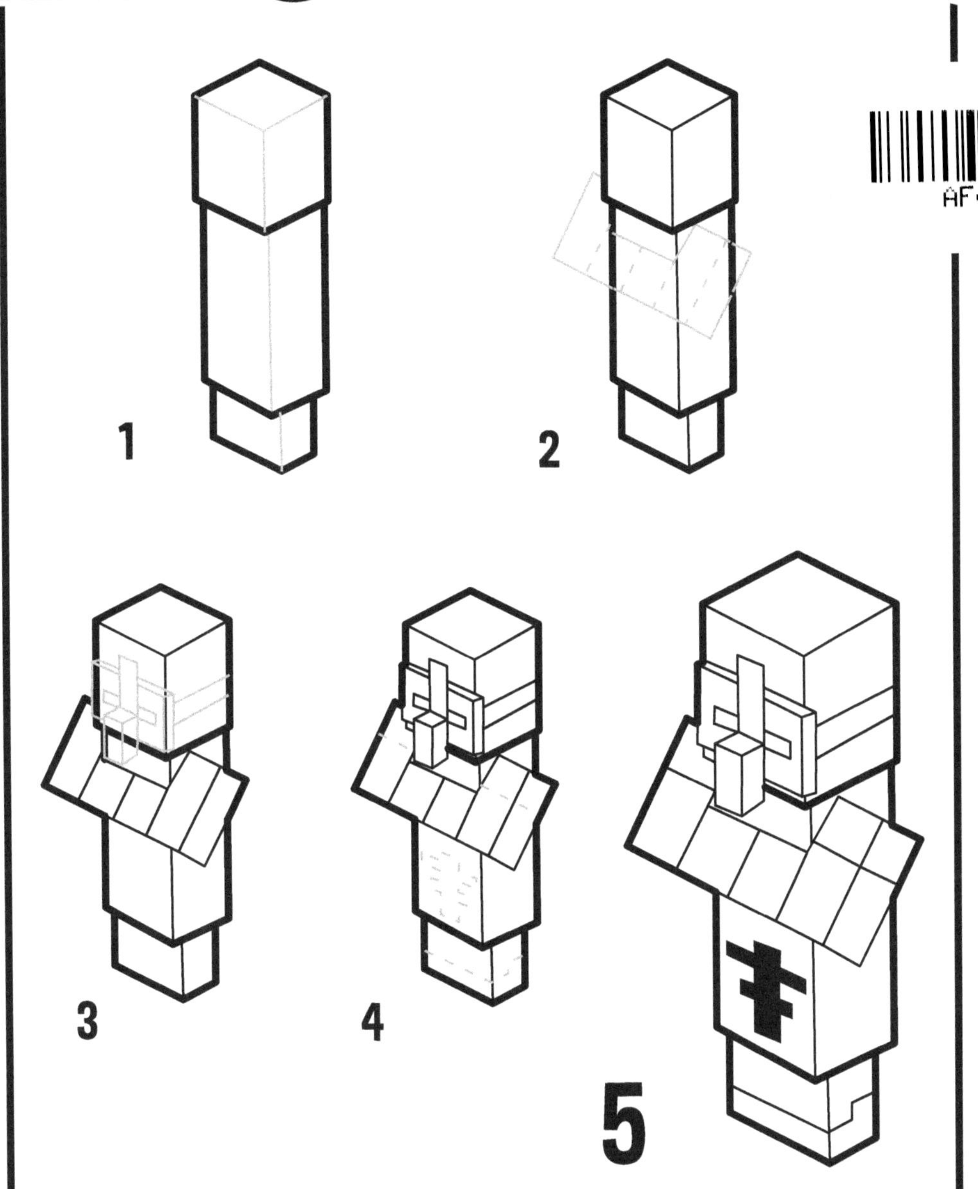

CUBE HUNTER

CUBE
HUNTER
WWW.CUBEHUNTER.NET

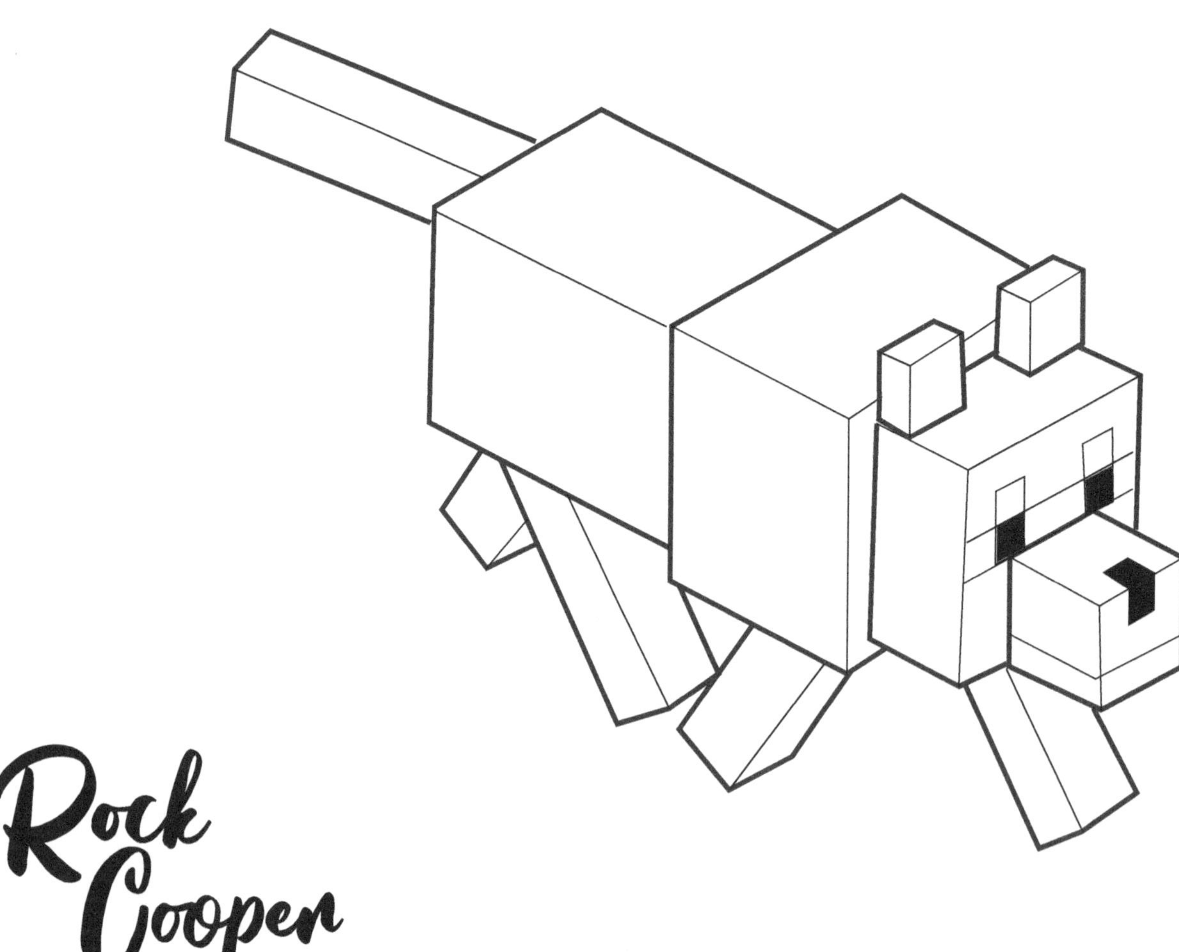

This Book Belongs to:

Welcome to the start of the journey where you will learn to draw the world of Minecraft! We will start from the simple most easy forms moving towards more complex characters! Here are presented the few tools you will need to accomplish great results... no worries it is nothing special only things that lay around the house! Yay! Can't wait to start!

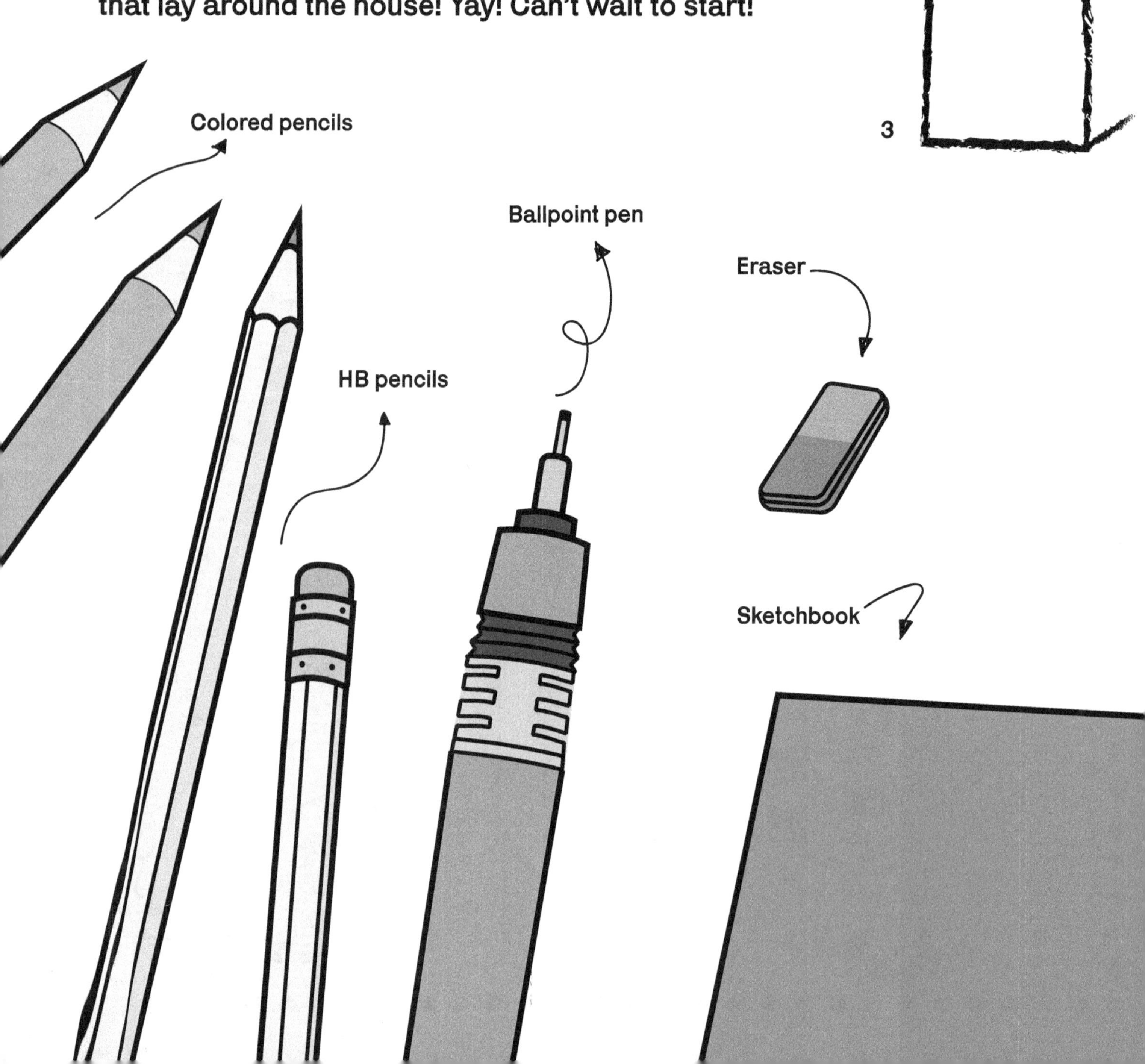

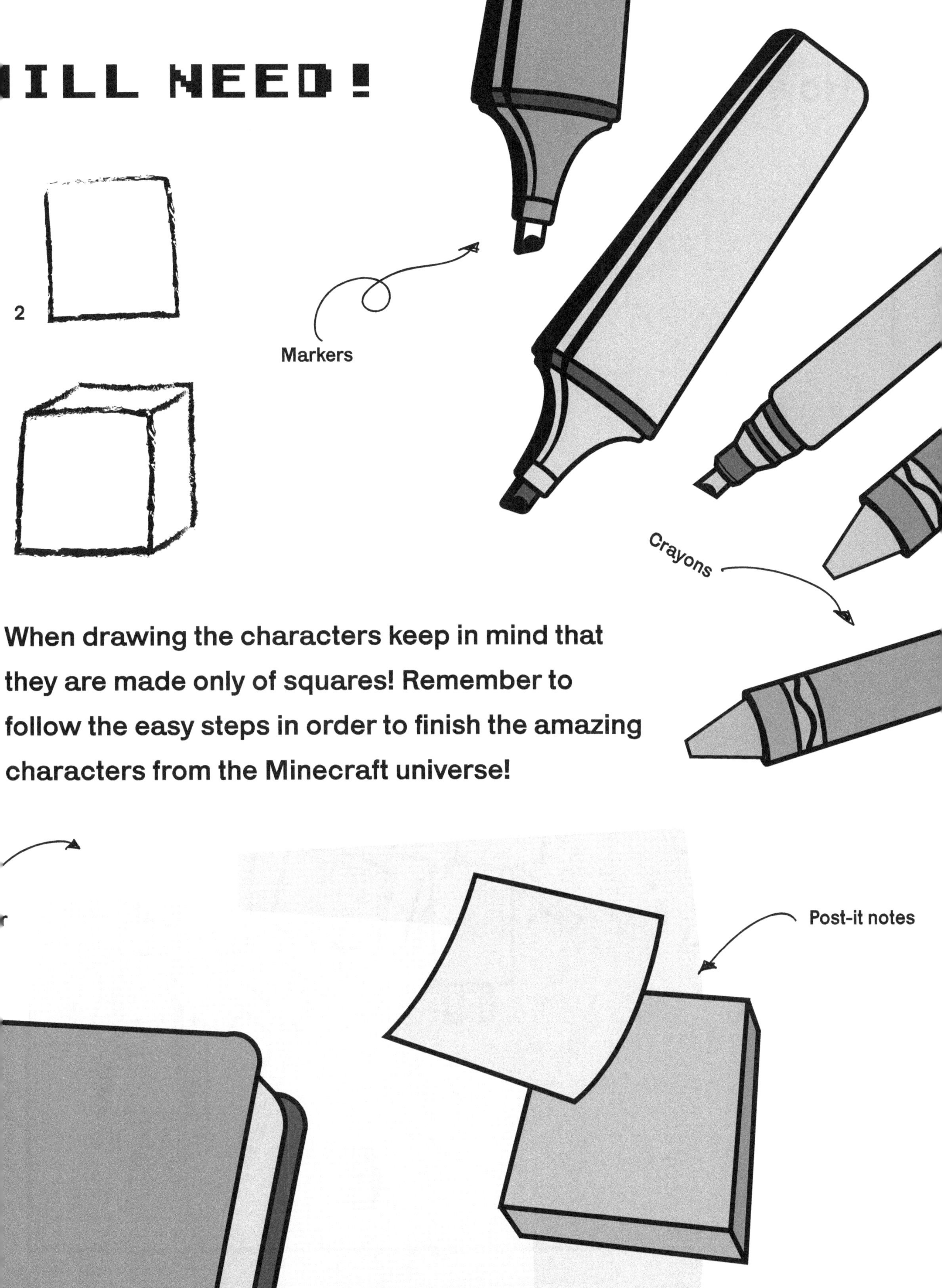

When drawing the characters keep in mind that they are made only of squares! Remember to follow the easy steps in order to finish the amazing characters from the Minecraft universe!

How to draw: Arch-Illager

1

2

3

4

5

6

Now, it's your turn

How to draw: Axe

1

2

3

4

5

Now, it's your turn

How to draw: Axel

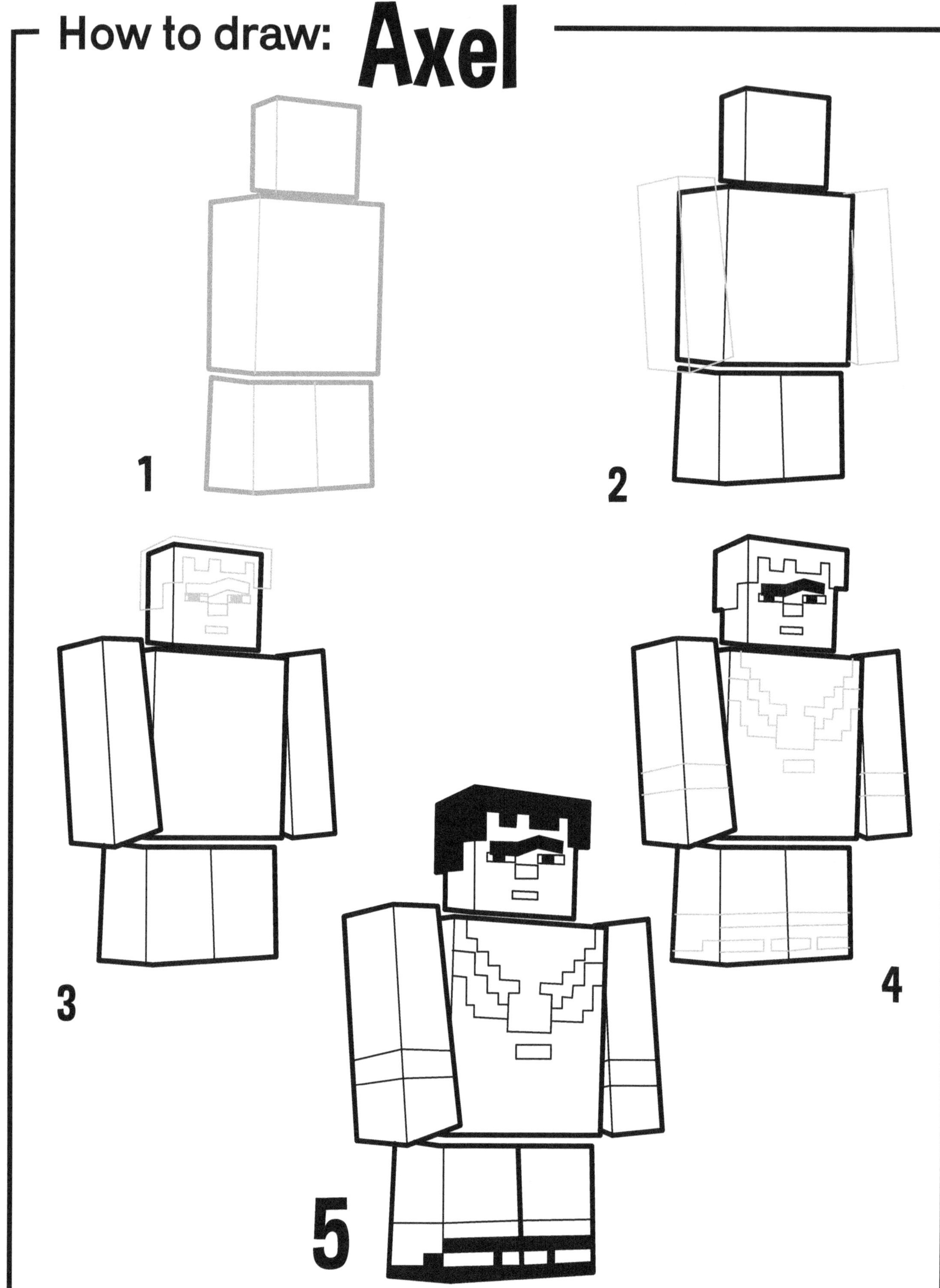

Now, it's your turn

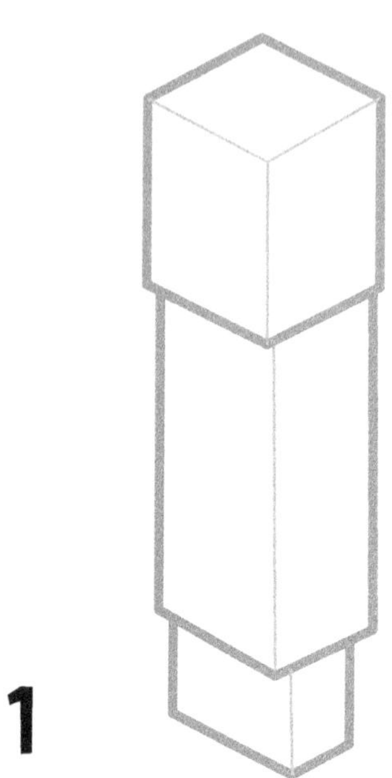

1

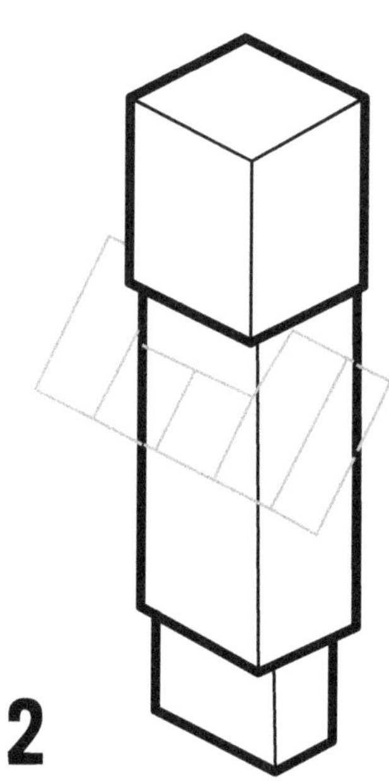

2

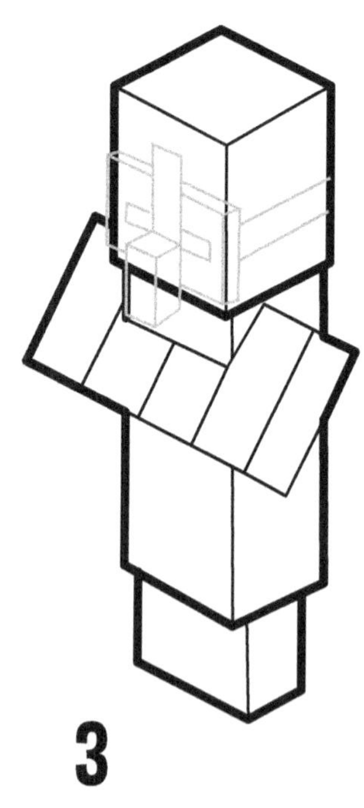

3

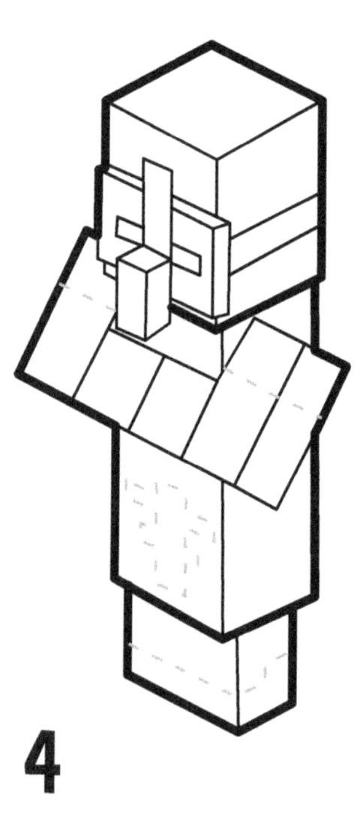

4

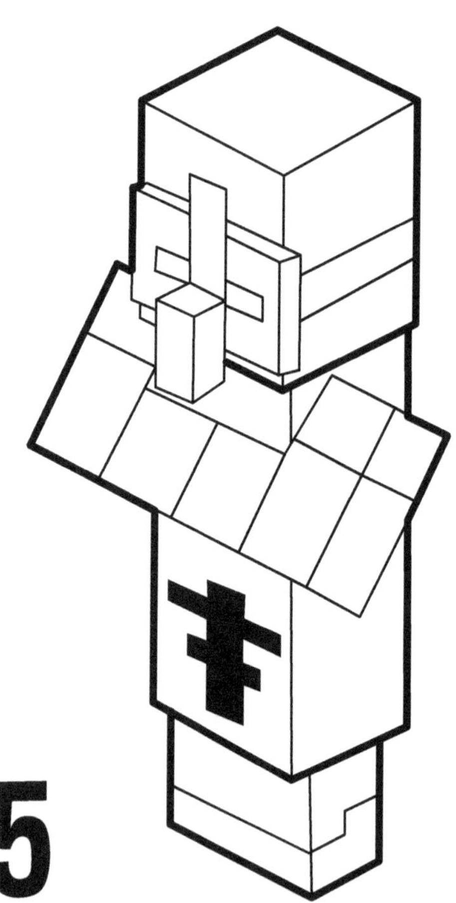

5

Now, it's your turn

How to draw: **Bow**

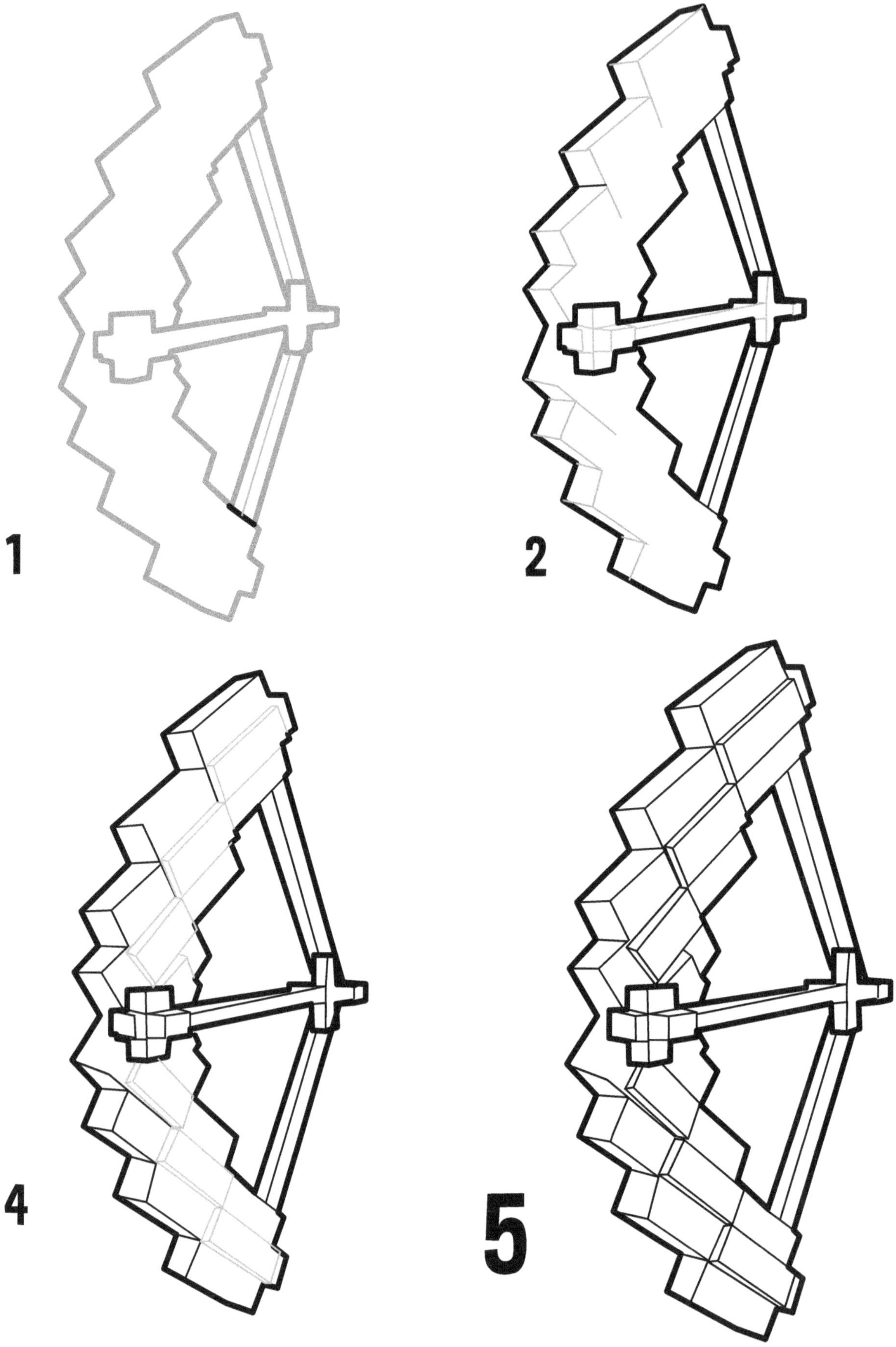

1

2

4

5

Now, it's your turn

How to draw: **Broadsword** 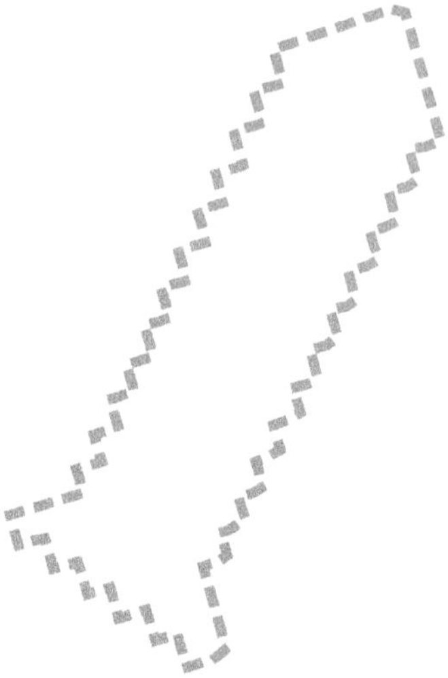
1 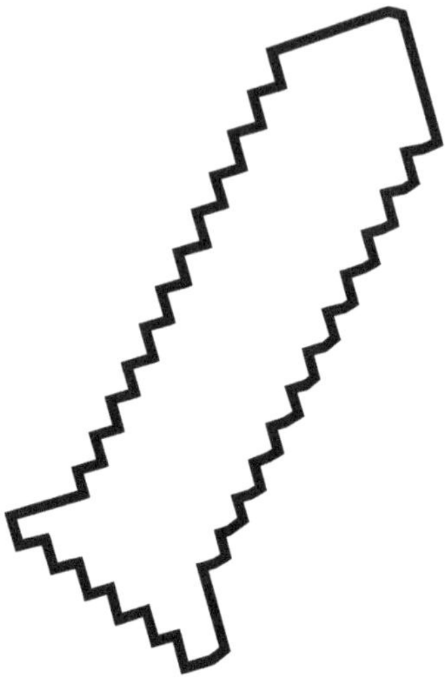
2 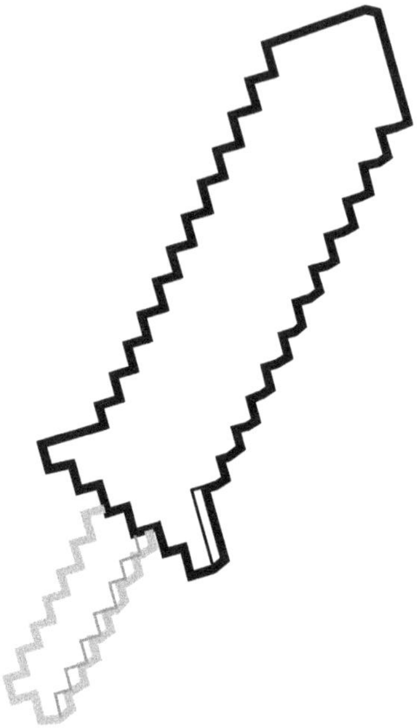
3 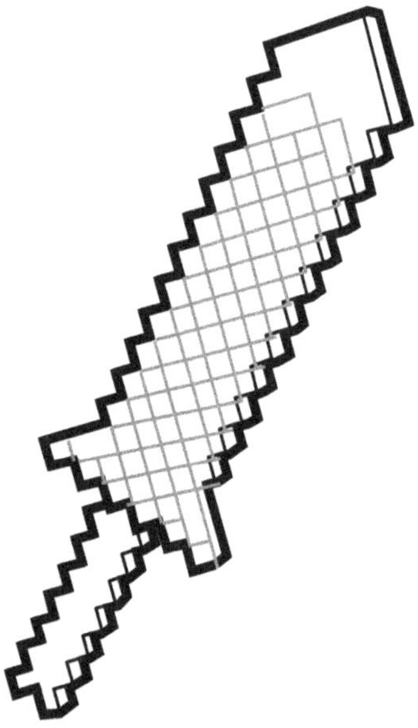
4 
5

Now, it's your turn

How to draw: **Corrupted Cauldron**

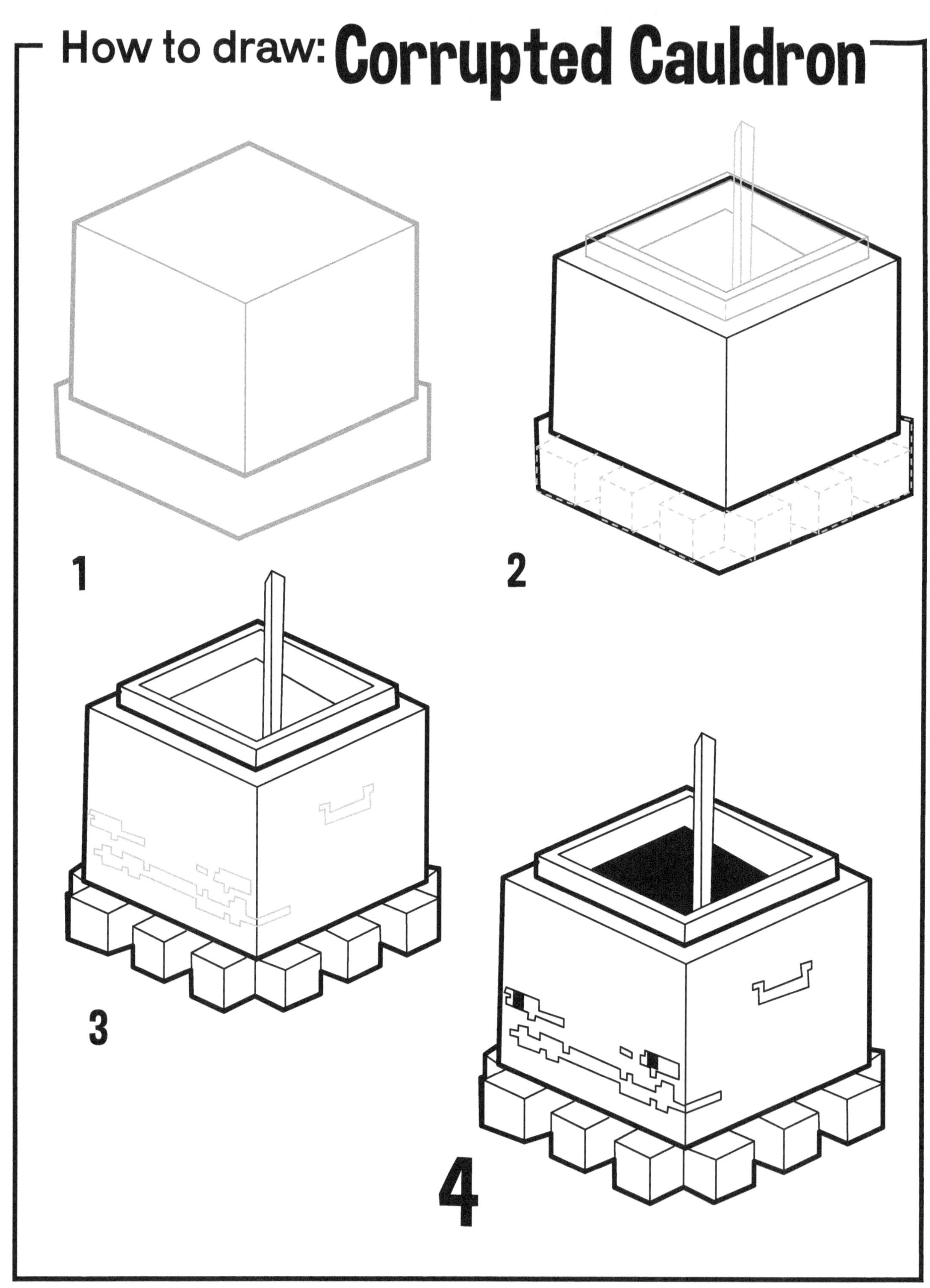

Now, it's your turn

How to draw: Corppupted Beacon

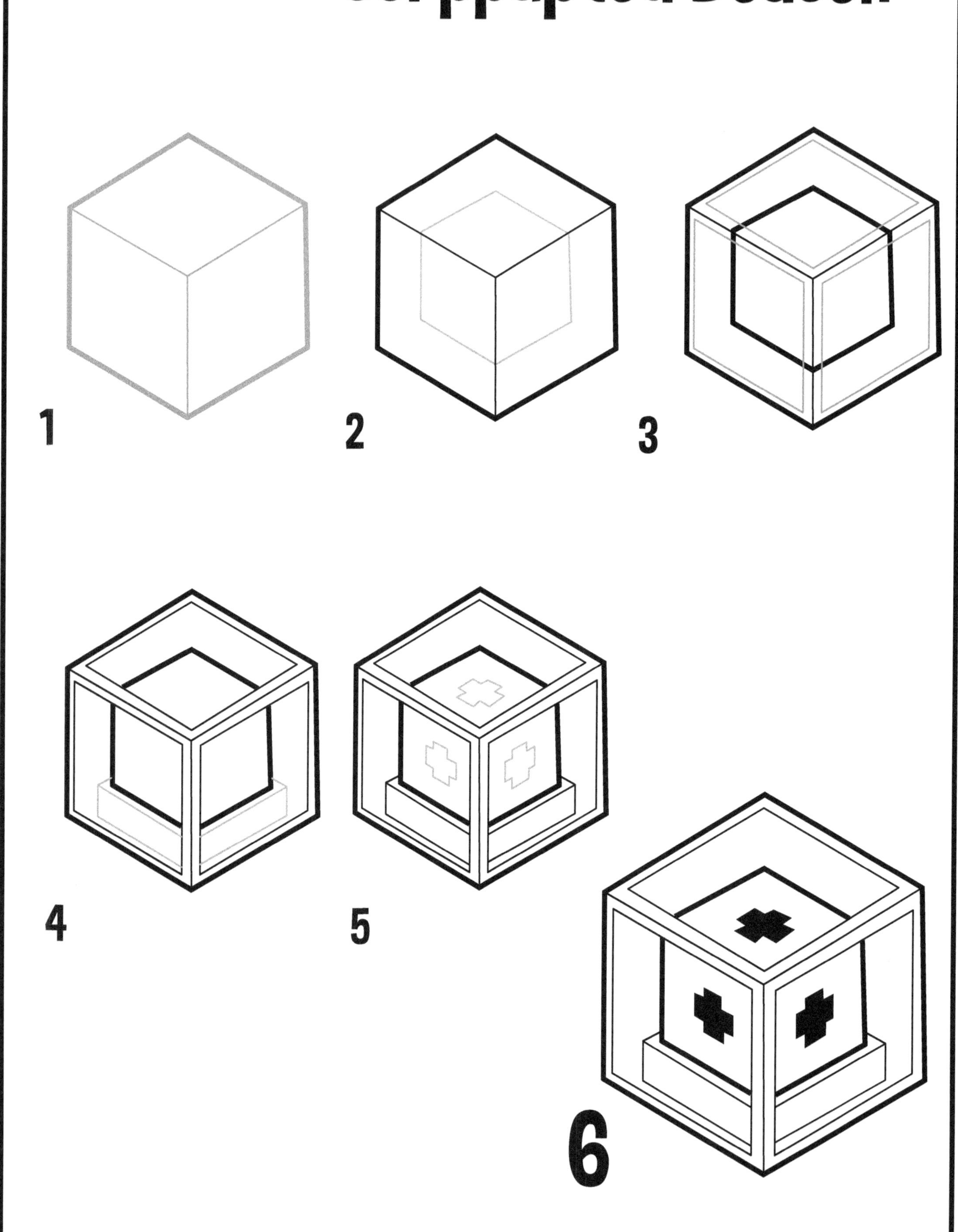

Now, it's your turn

How to draw: Dolphin

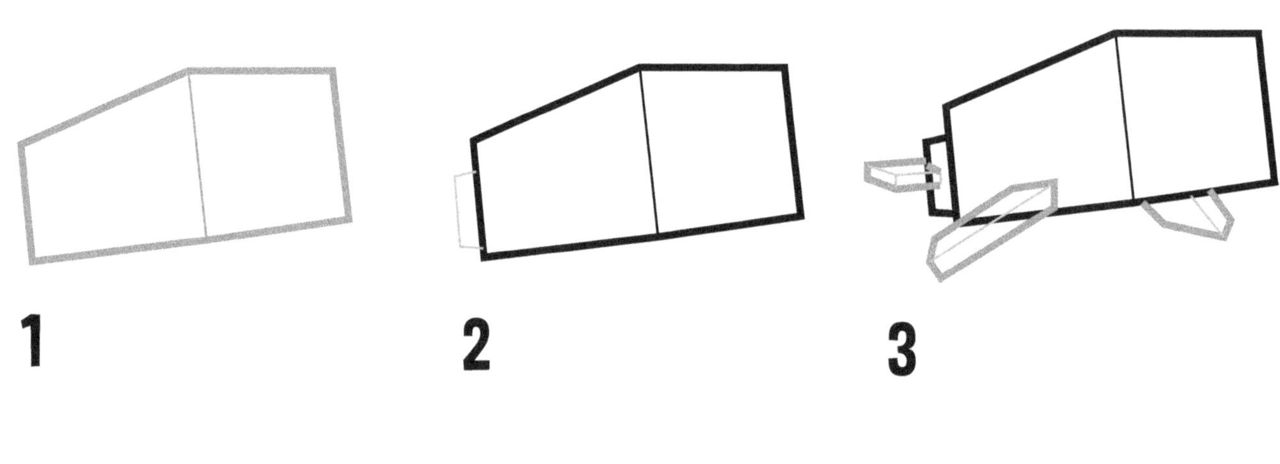

1   **2**   **3**

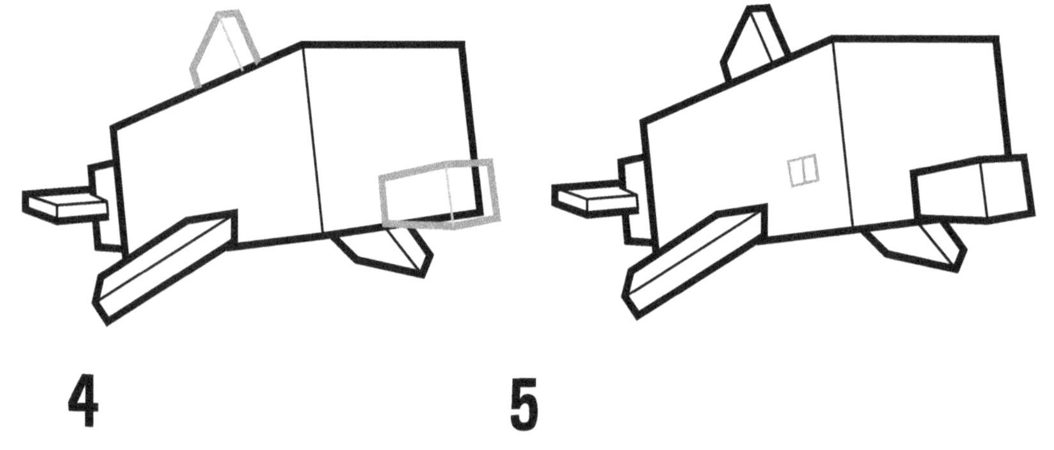

4   **5**

6

Now, it's your turn

How to draw: Ellegaard

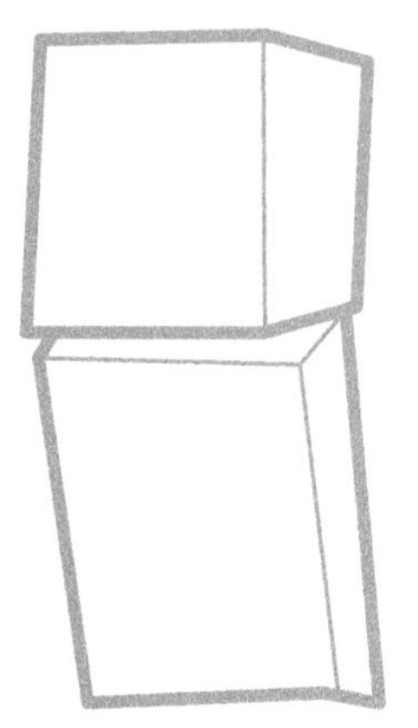

1

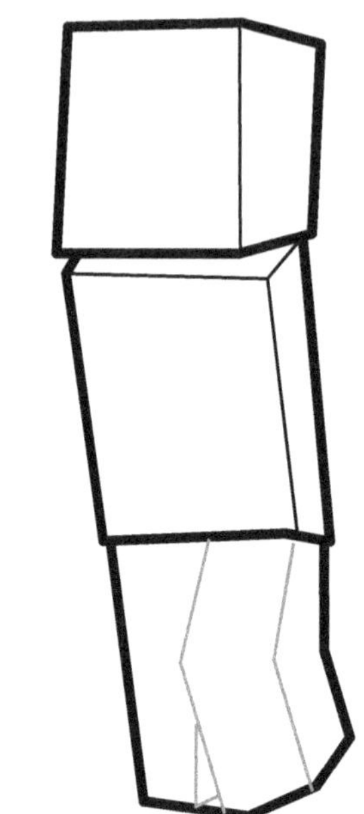

2

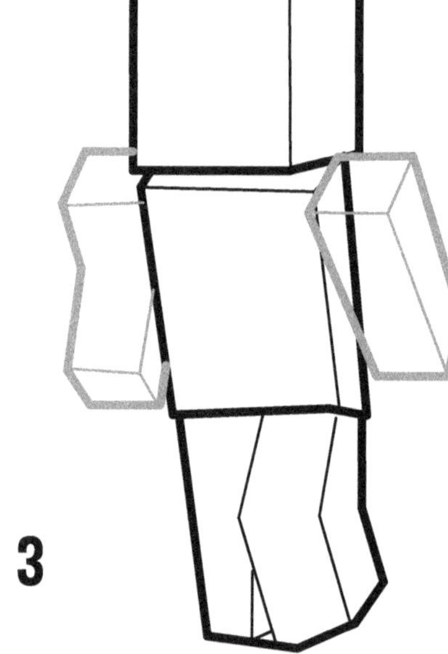

3

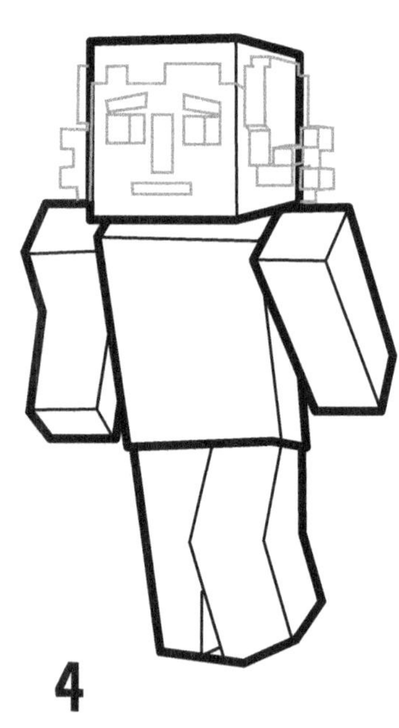

4

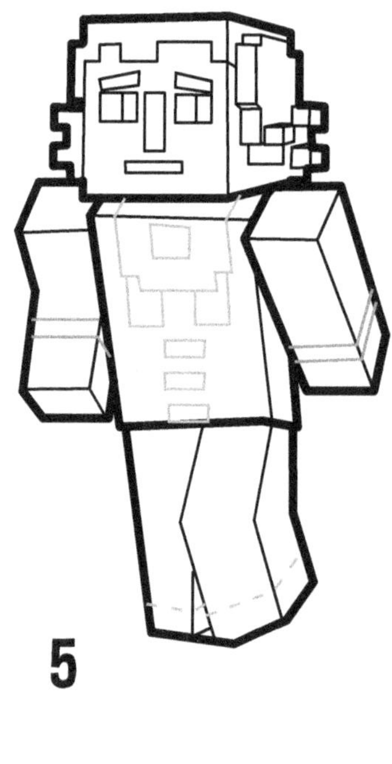

5

6

Now, it's your turn

How to draw: Enchanter

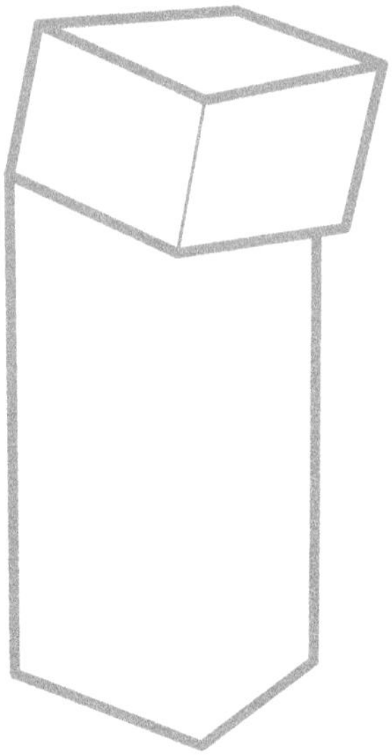

1

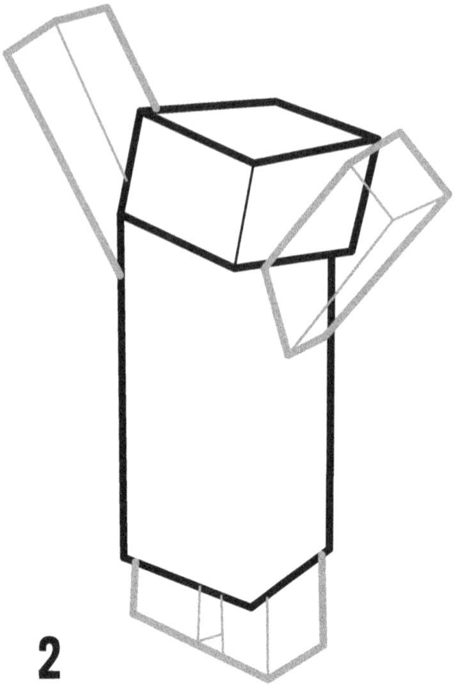

2

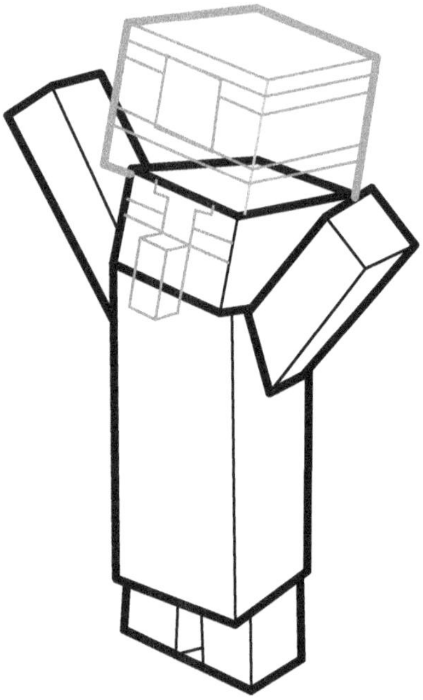

3

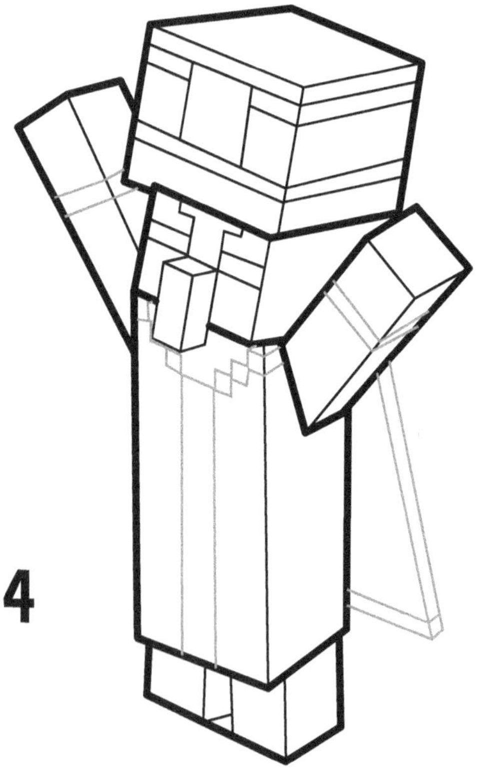

4

5

Now, it's your turn

How to draw:  Fox

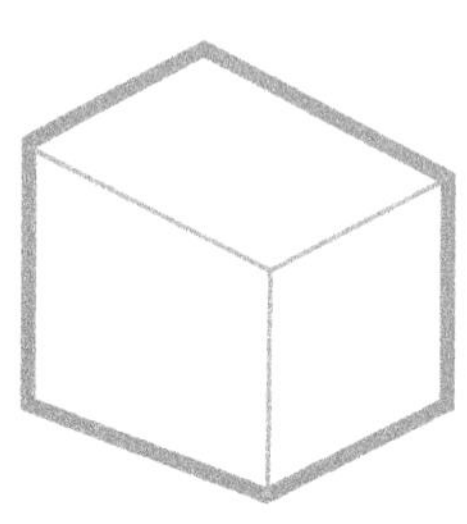

1

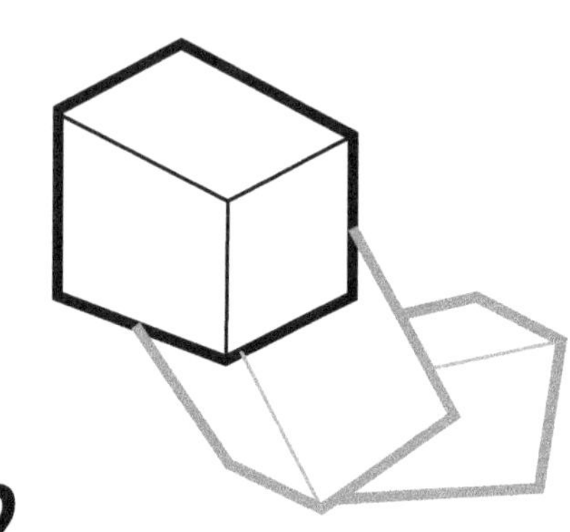

2

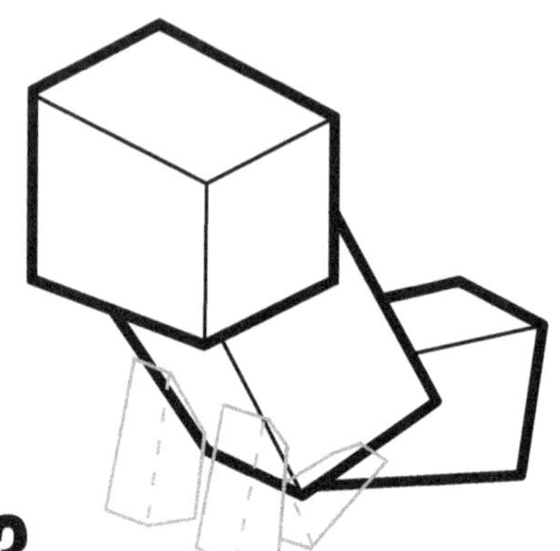

3

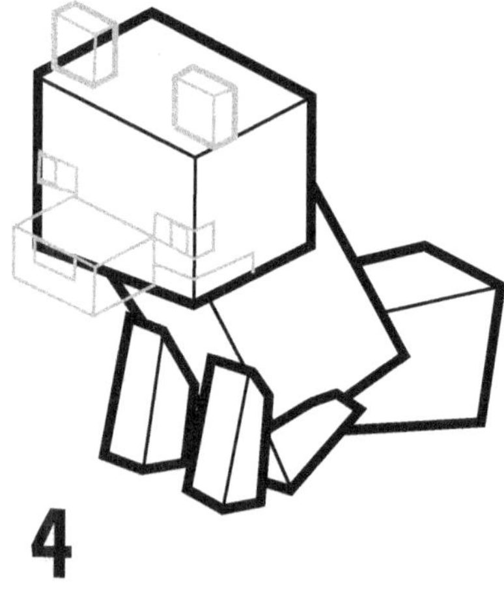

4

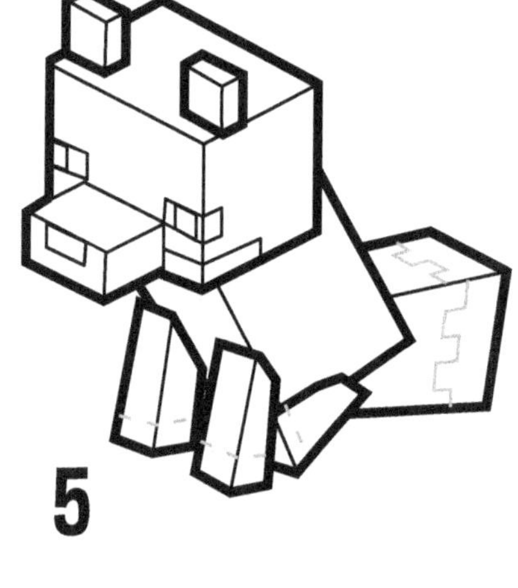

5

6

Now, it's your turn

How to draw: **Gabriel**

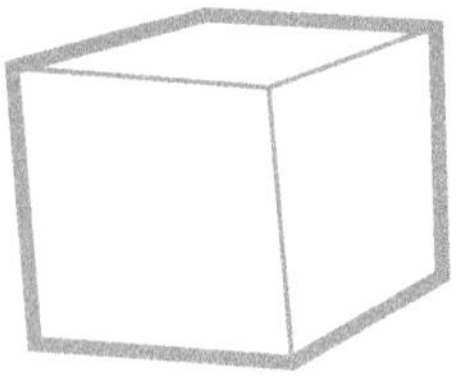

1

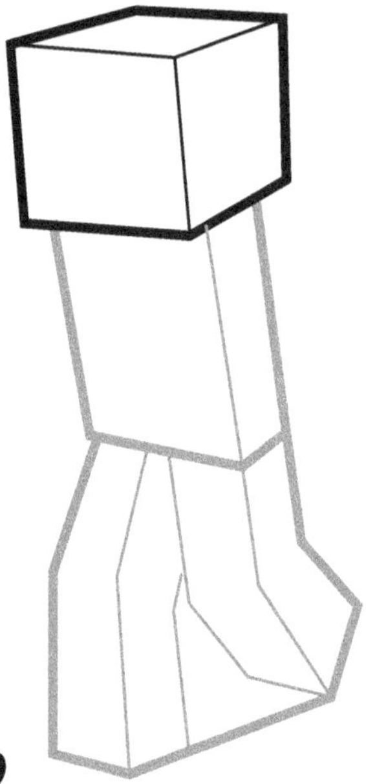

2

3

4

5

6

Now, it's your turn

How to draw: Great Hammer

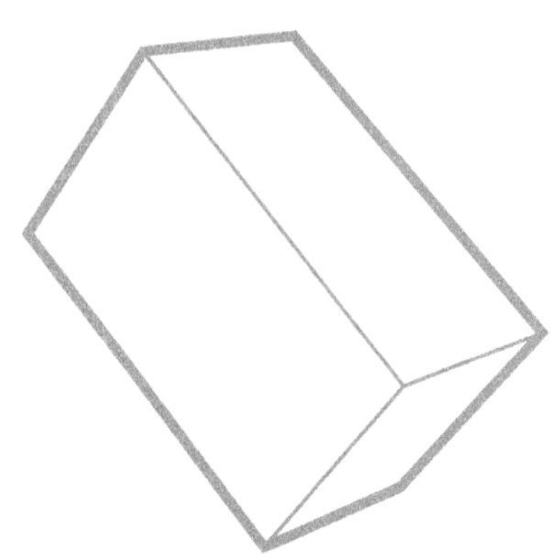

1

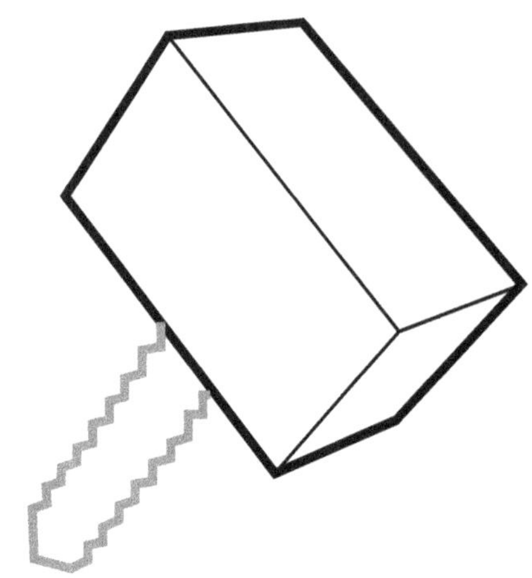

2

3

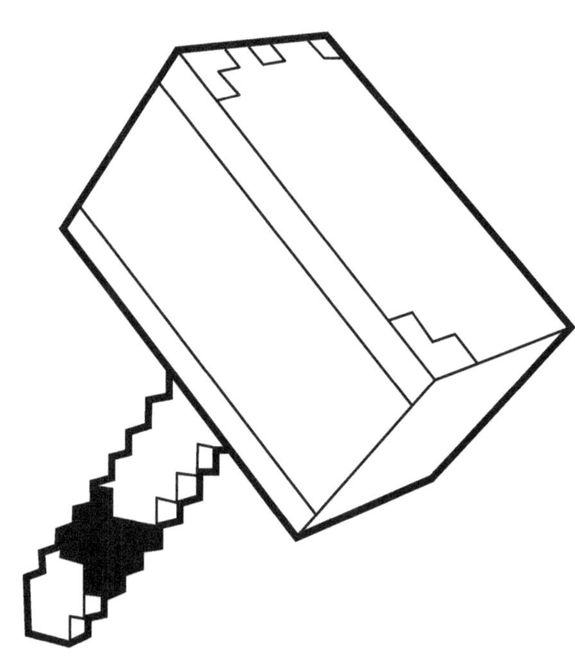

4

Now, it's your turn

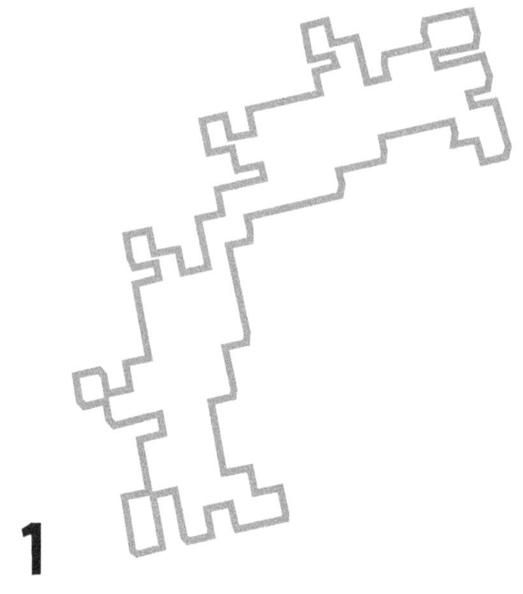

1

2

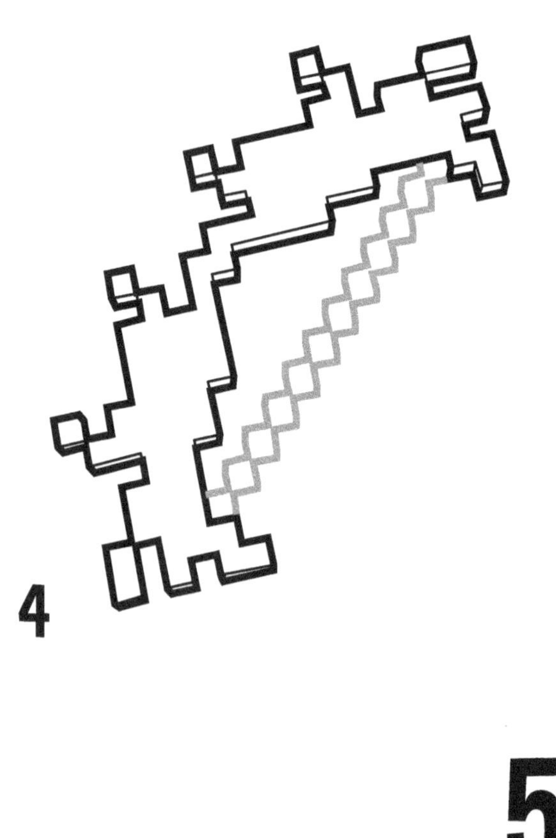

4

5

Now, it's your turn

How to draw: Ice Wand

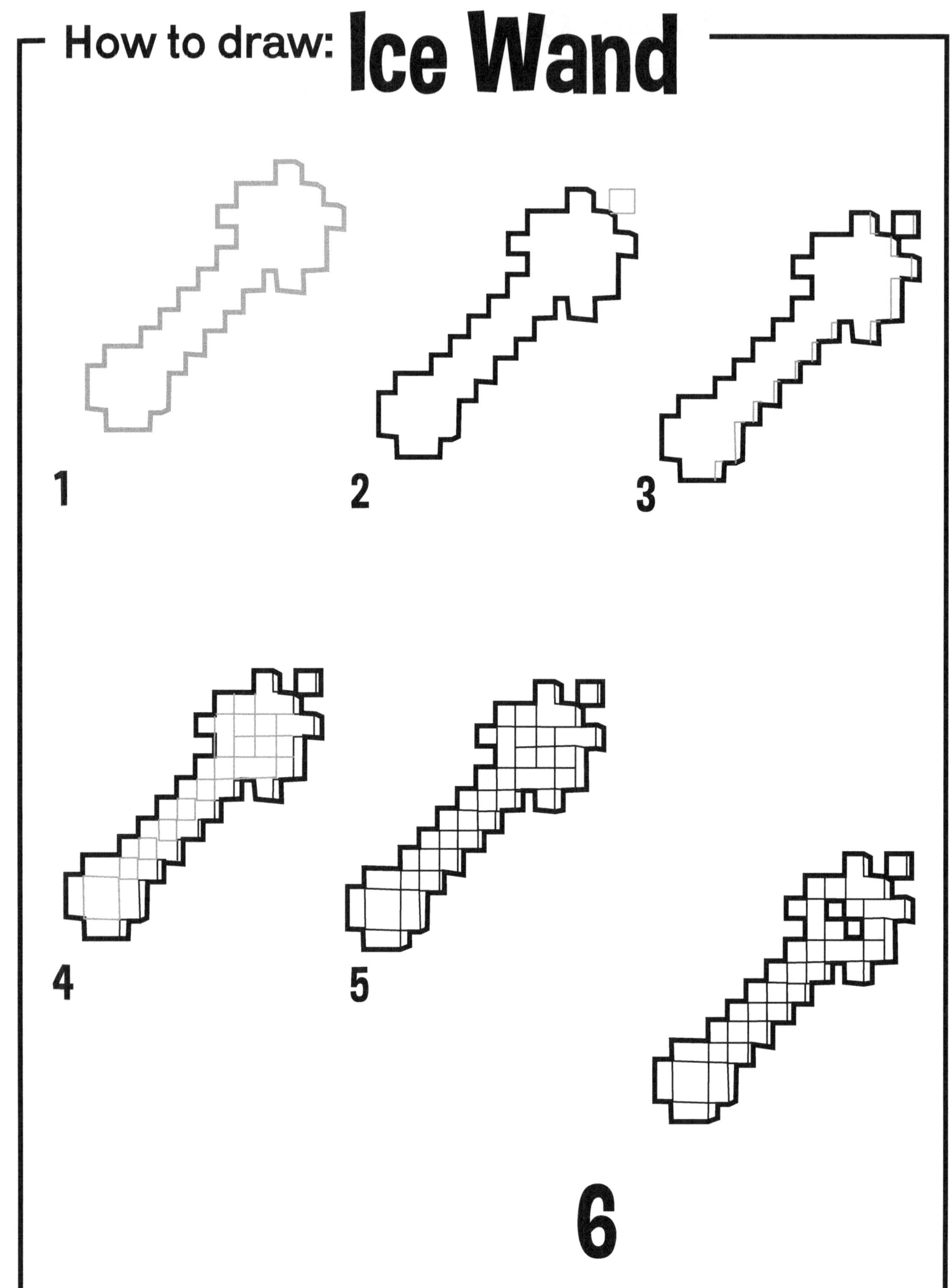

Now, it's your turn

How to draw: Ivor

1

2

3

4

5

6

Now, it's your turn

How to draw: Jess

1

2

3

4

5

6

Now, it's your turn

How to draw: Jungle Abomination

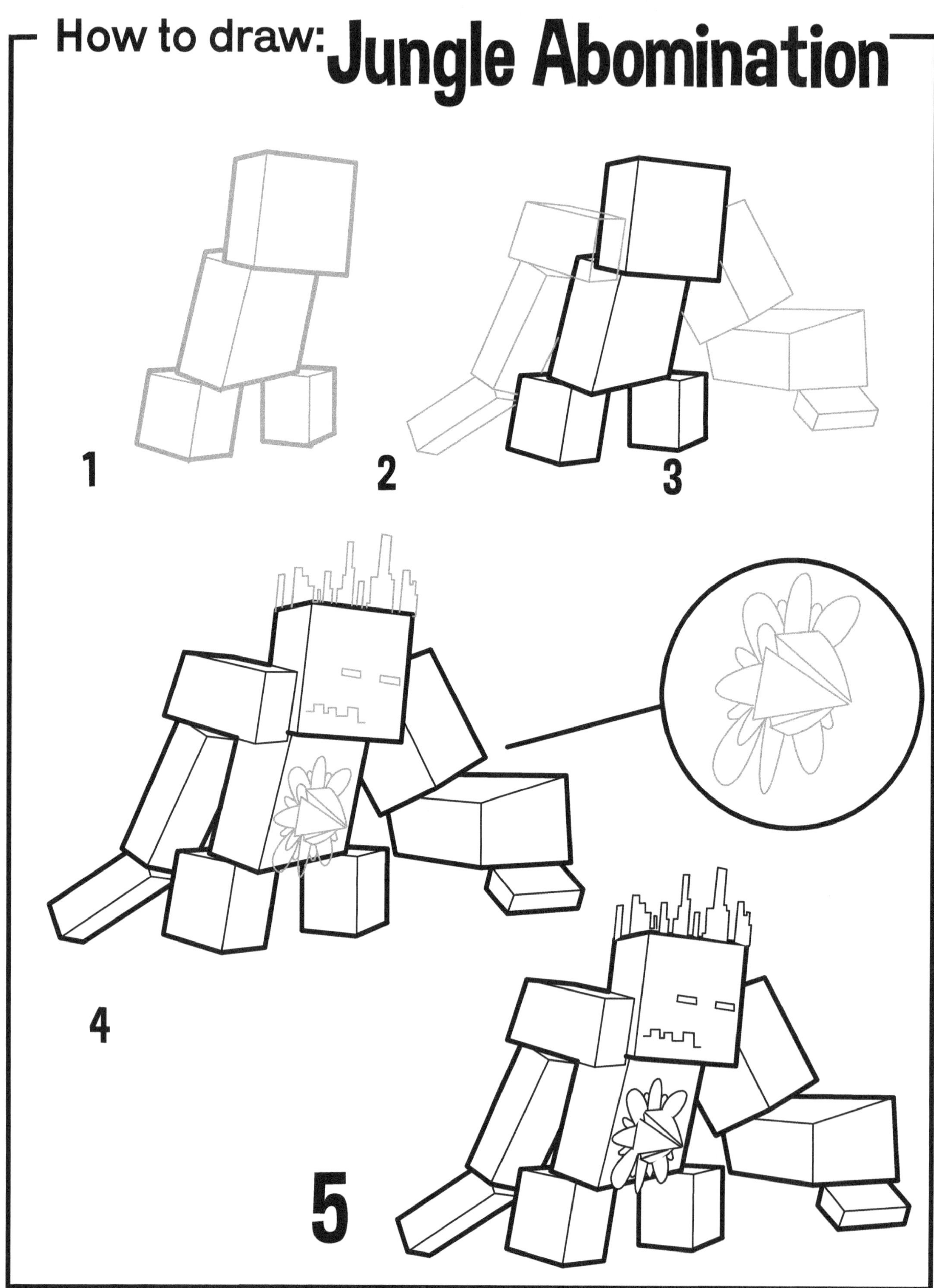

Now, it's your turn

How to draw: Light Feather

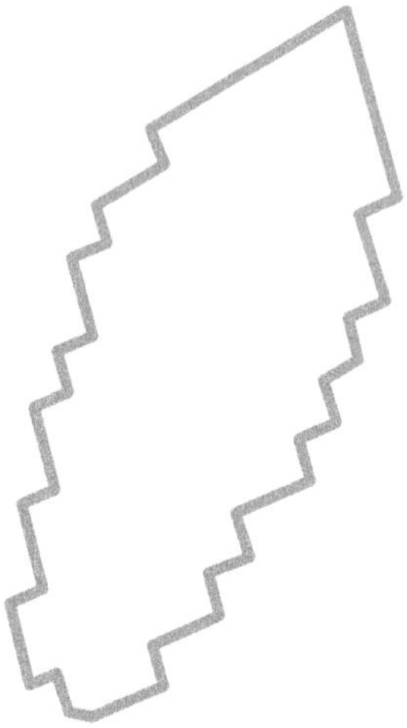

1

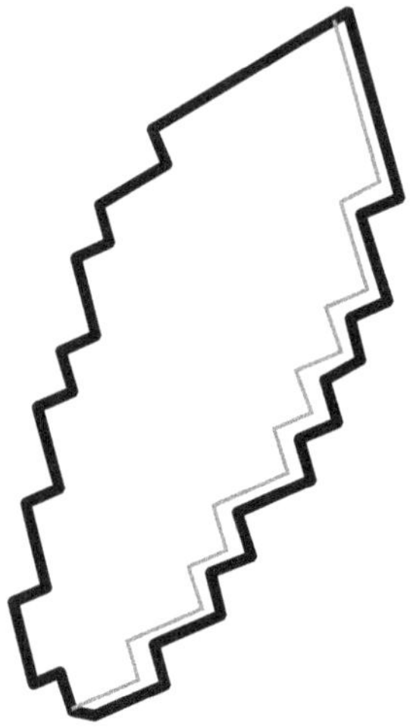

2

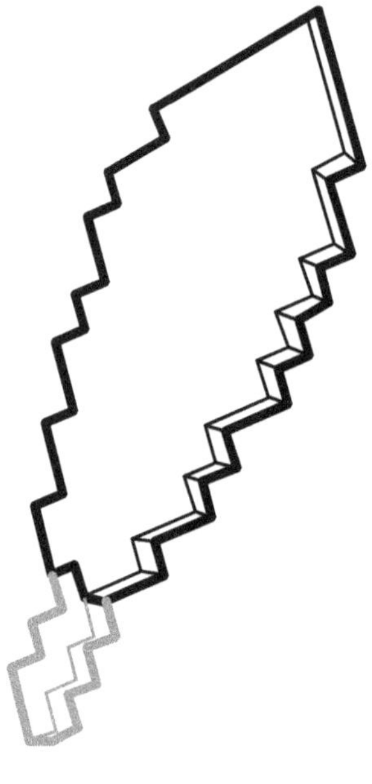

3

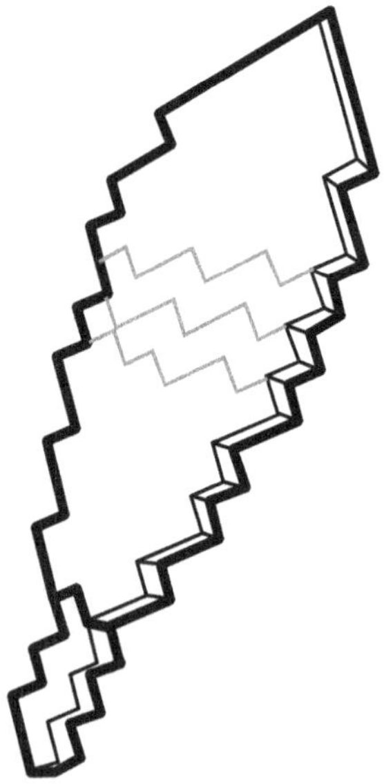

4

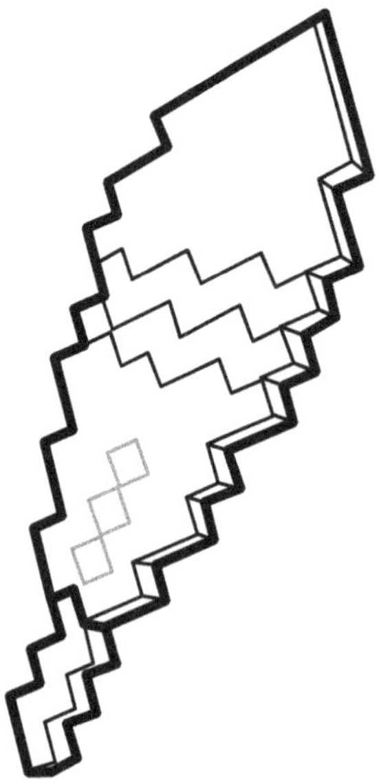

5

6

Now, it's your turn

How to draw: Lighning Rod 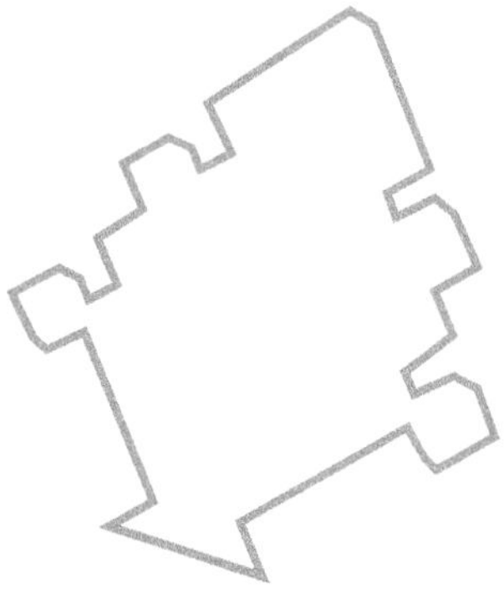
1 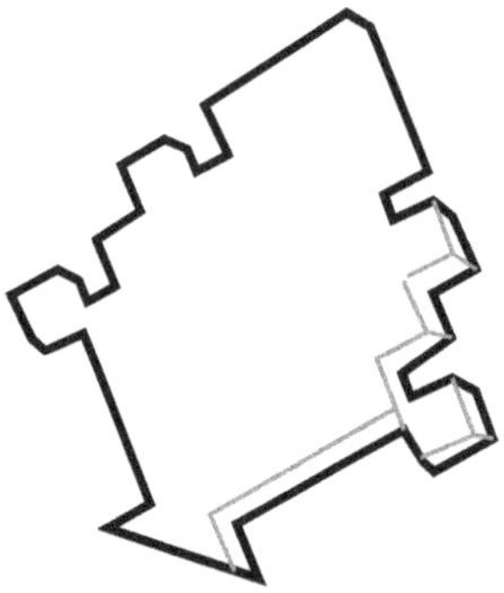
2 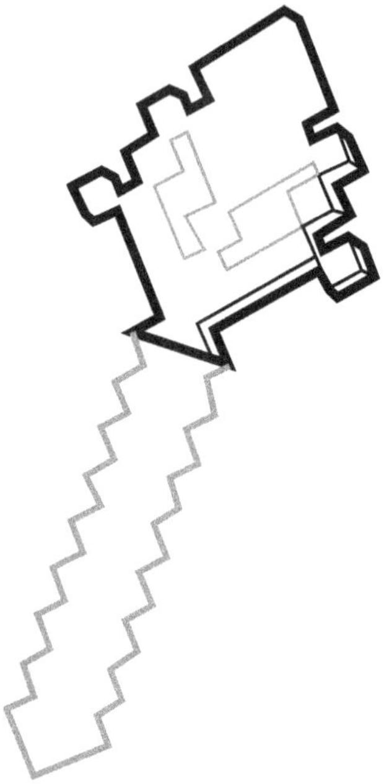
3 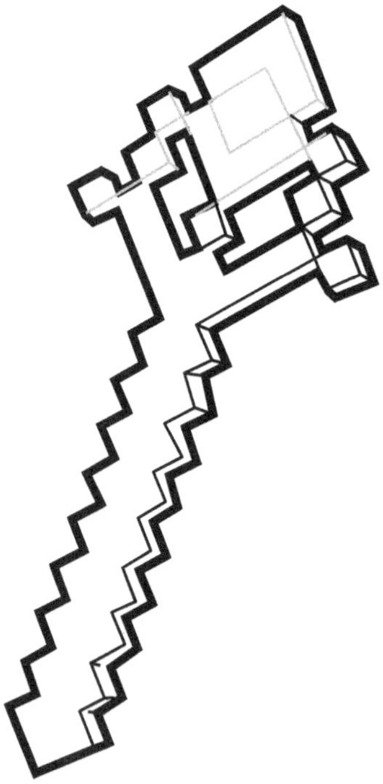
4 
5

Now, it's your turn

How to draw: Lukas

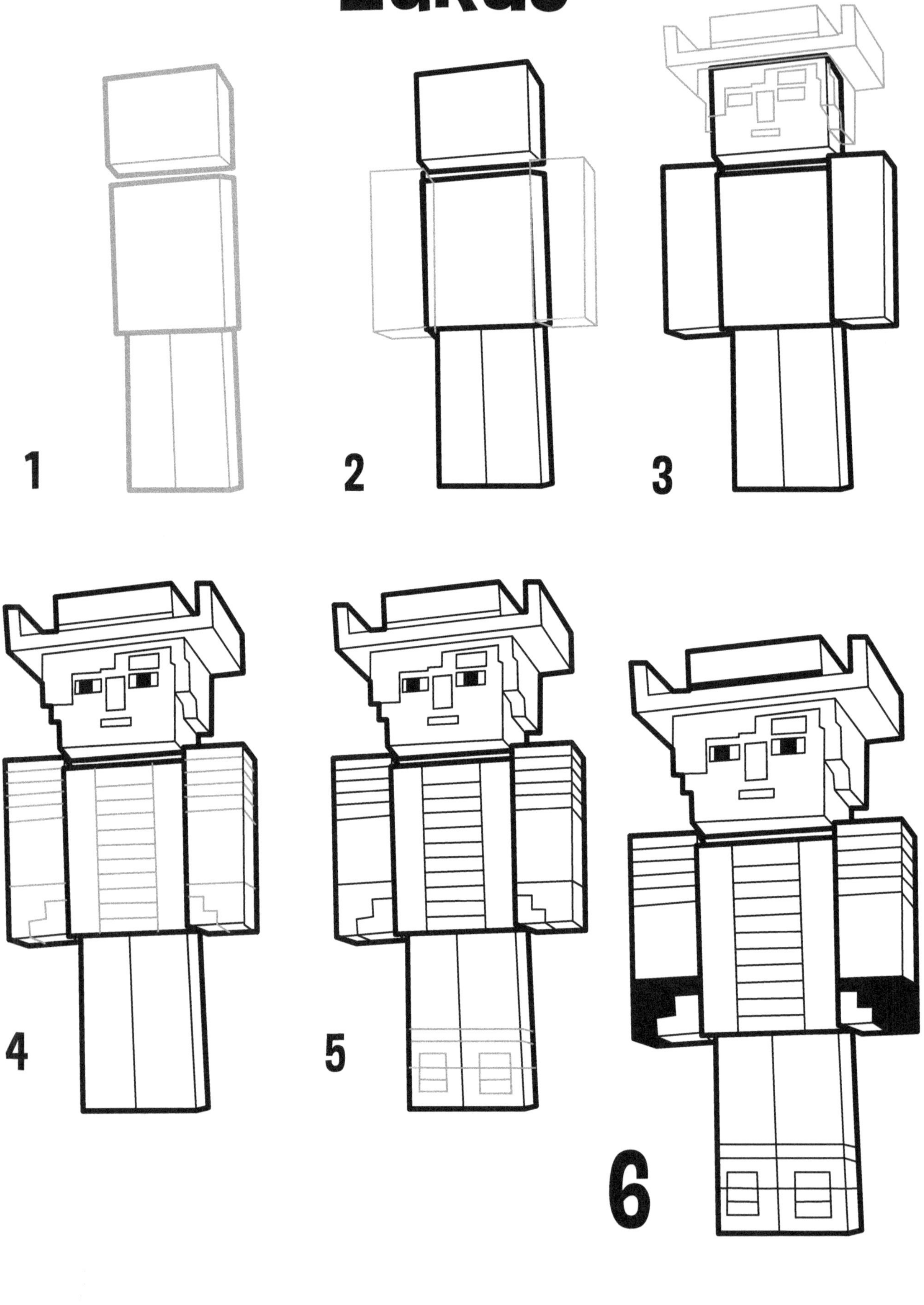

1

2

3

4

5

6

Now, it's your turn

How to draw: Luxury Merchant

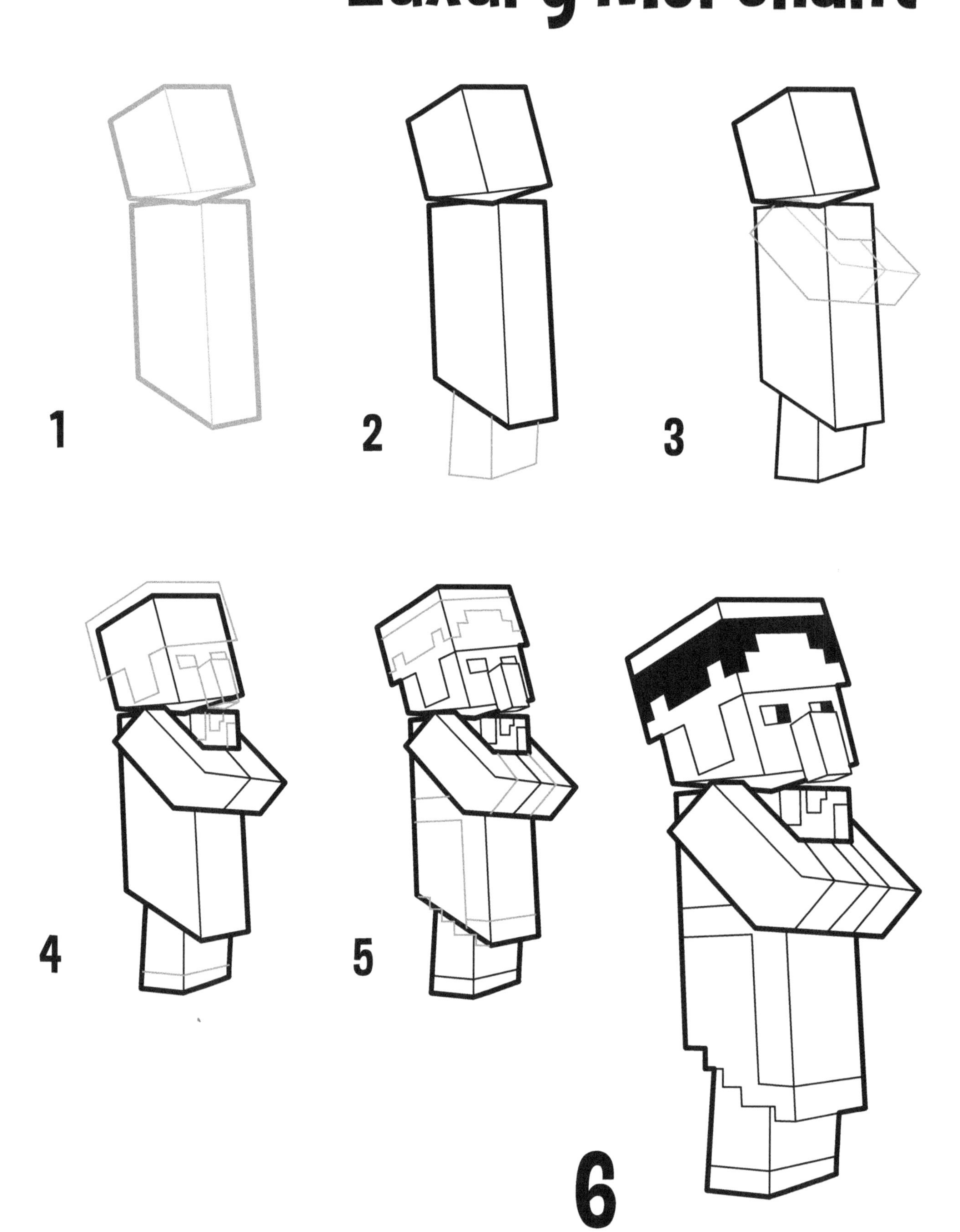

Now, it's your turn

How to draw: Mistery Merchant

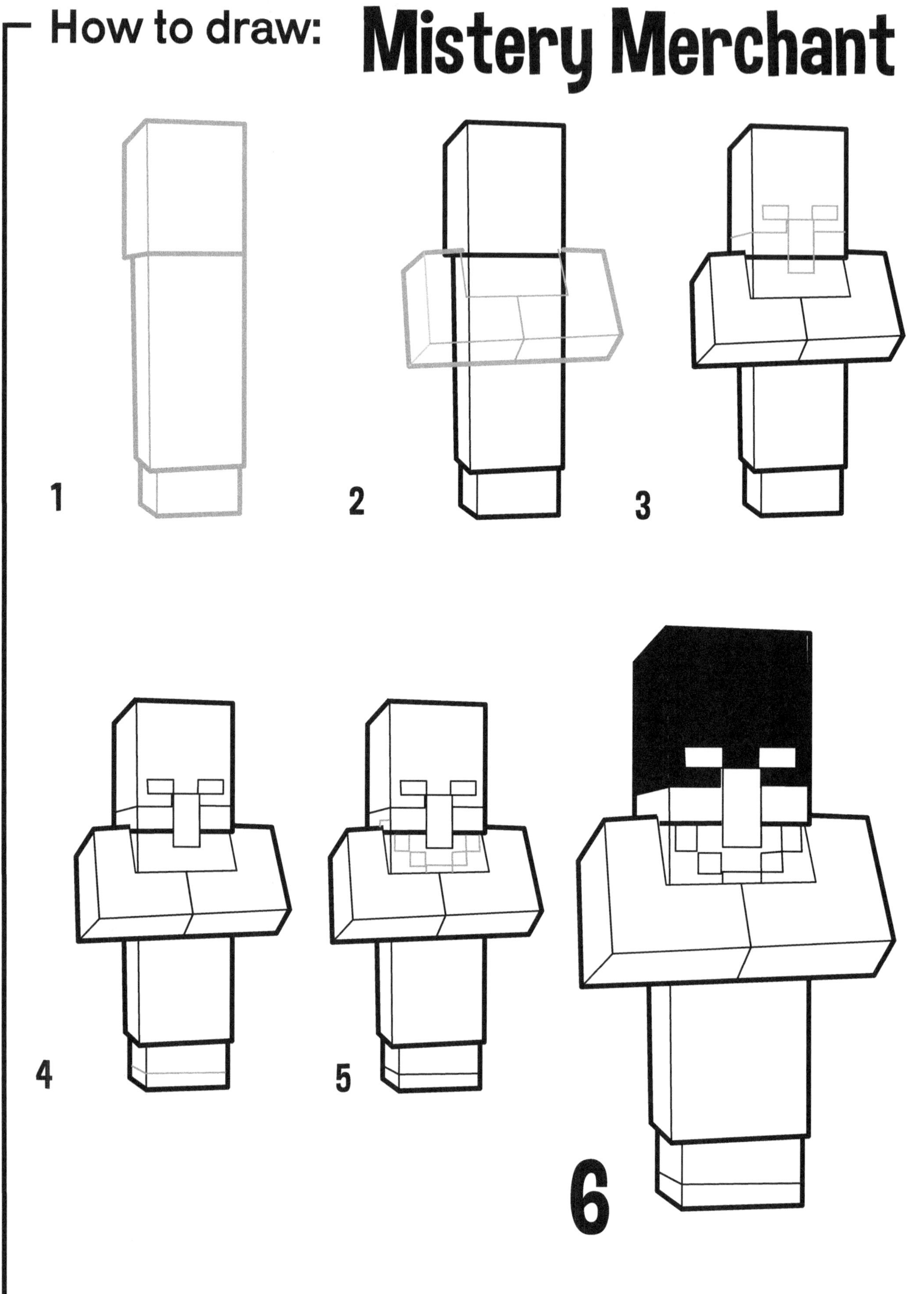

1
2
3
4
5
6

Now, it's your turn

How to draw: Mushroom Cow

1

2

3

4

5

Now, it's your turn

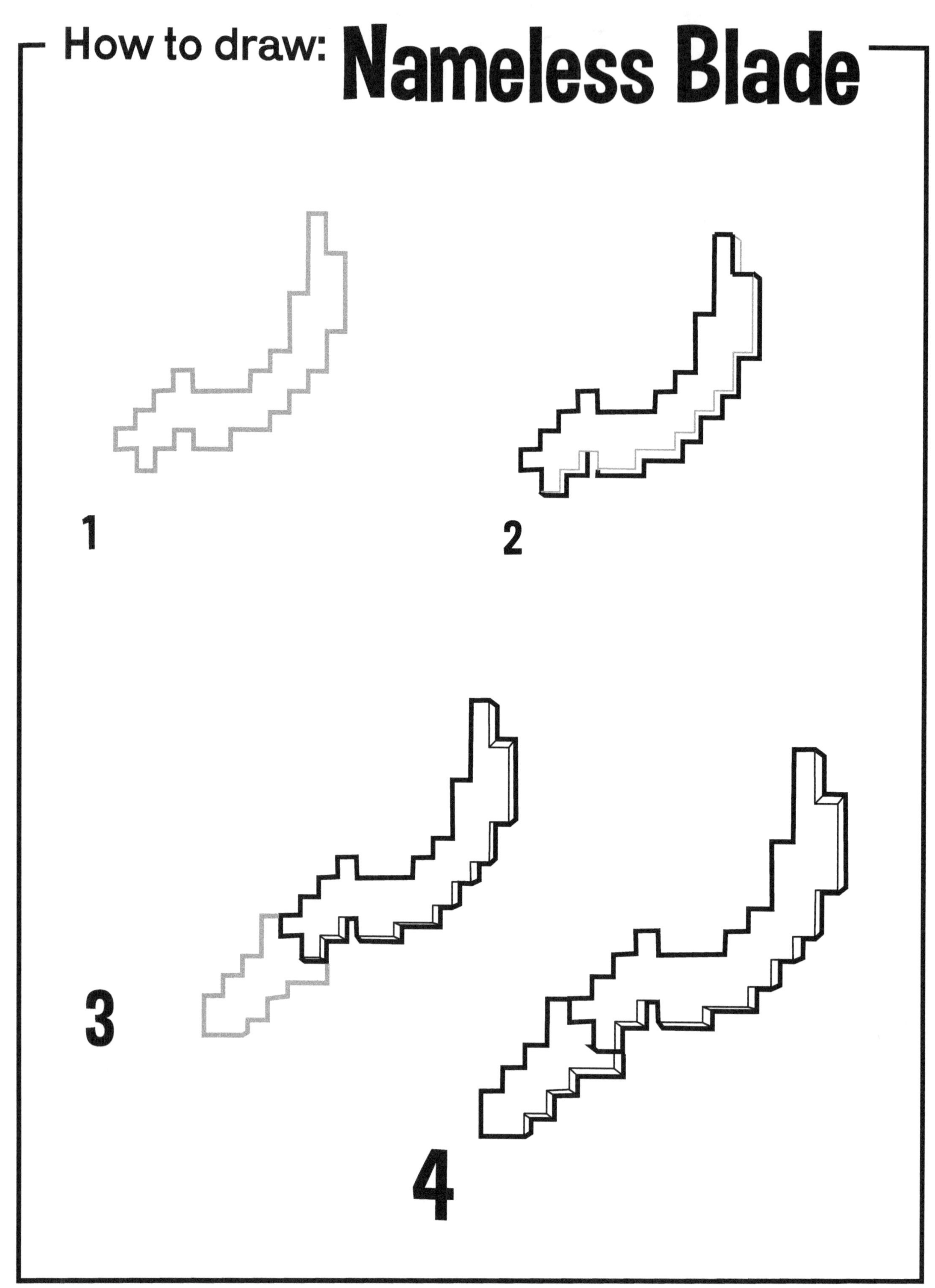

1
2
3
4

Now, it's your turn

How to draw: Nameless One

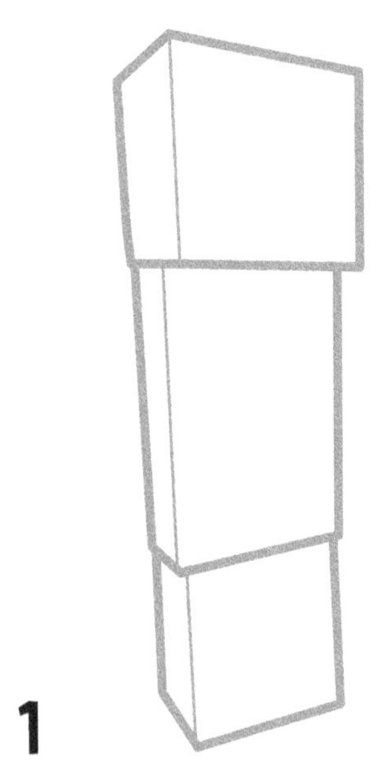

1

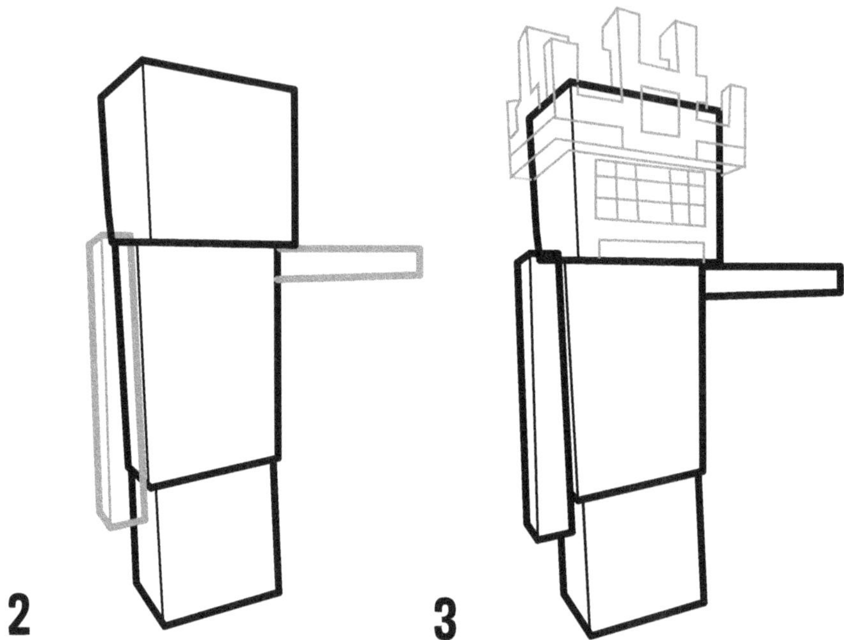

2

3

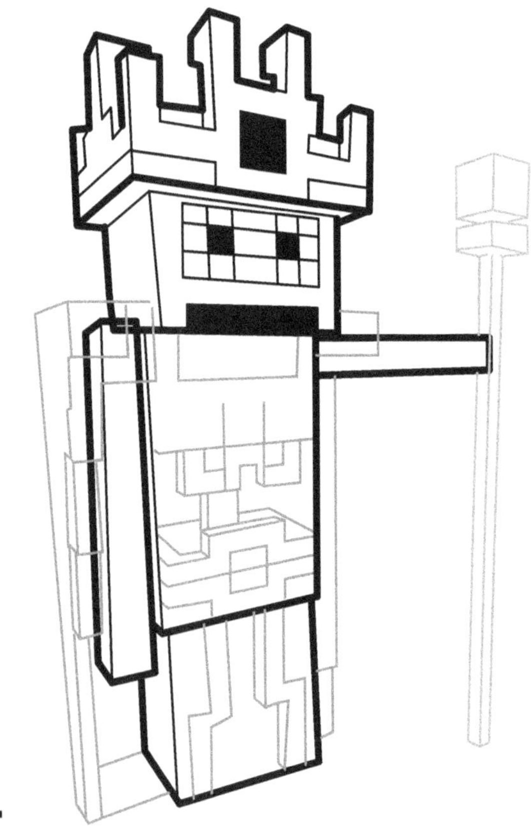

4

5

Now, it's your turn

How to draw: Necromancer

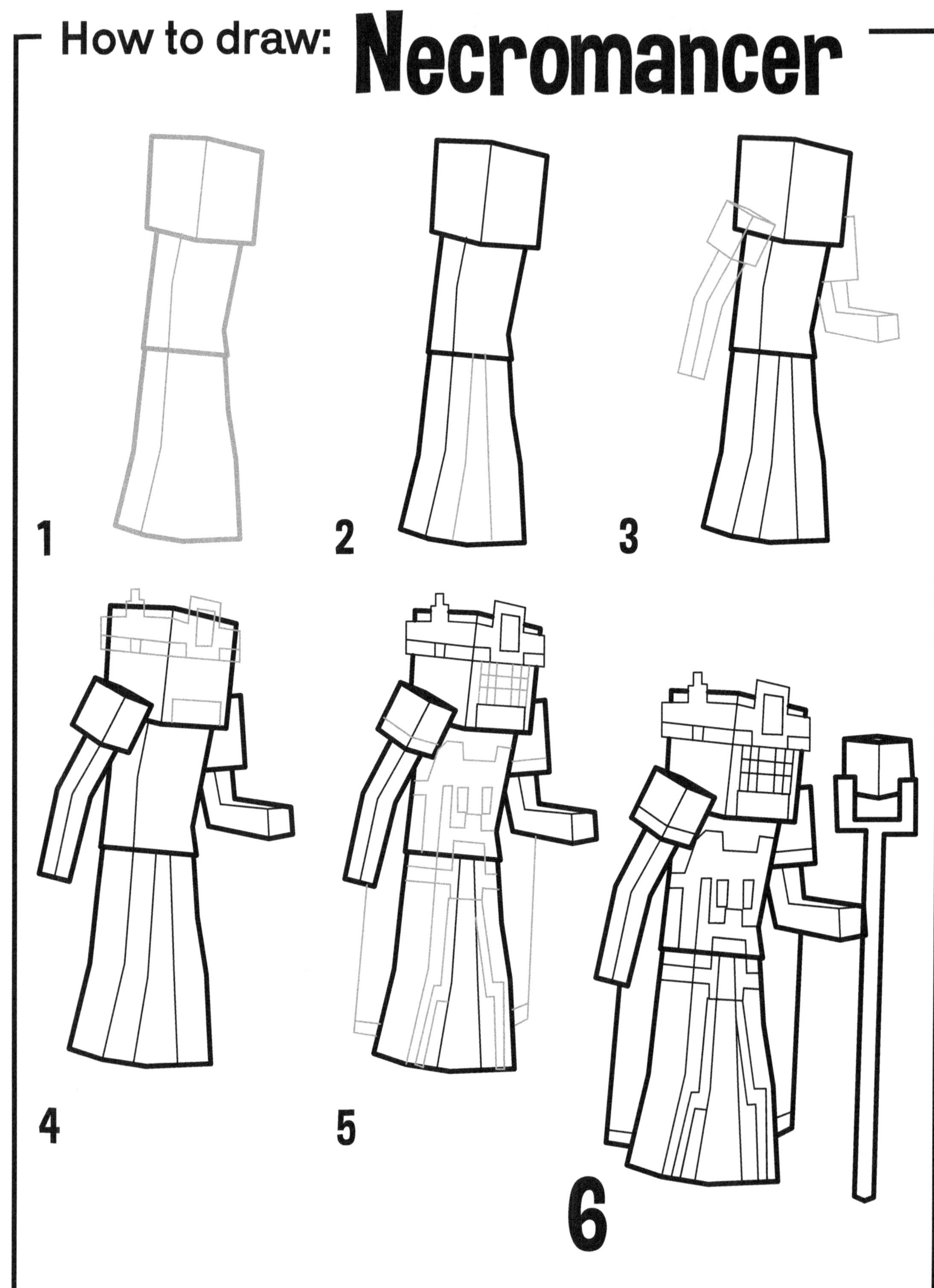

1
2
3
4
5
6

Now, it's your turn

1

2

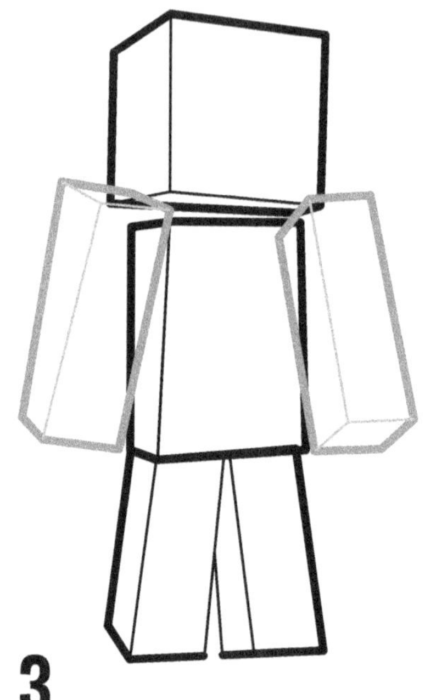

3

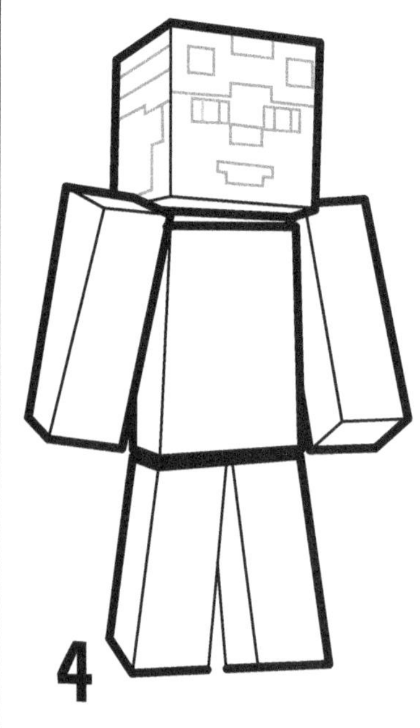

4

5

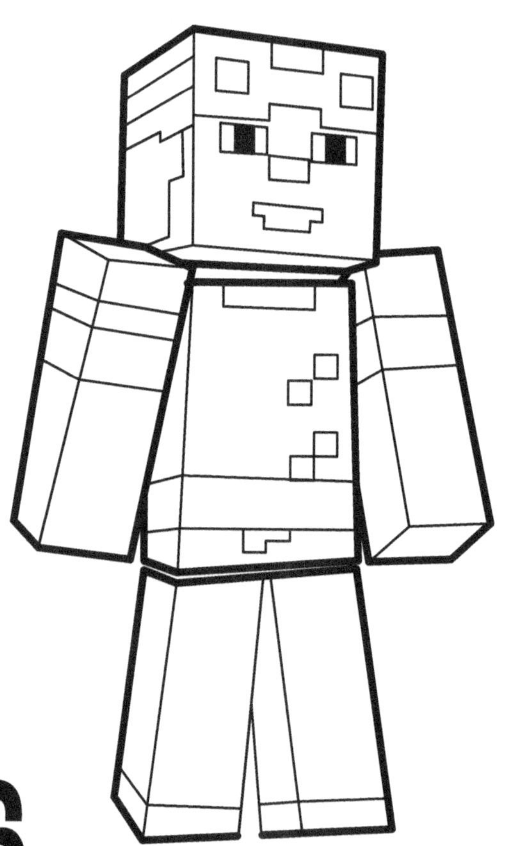

6

Now, it's your turn

How to draw: Panda

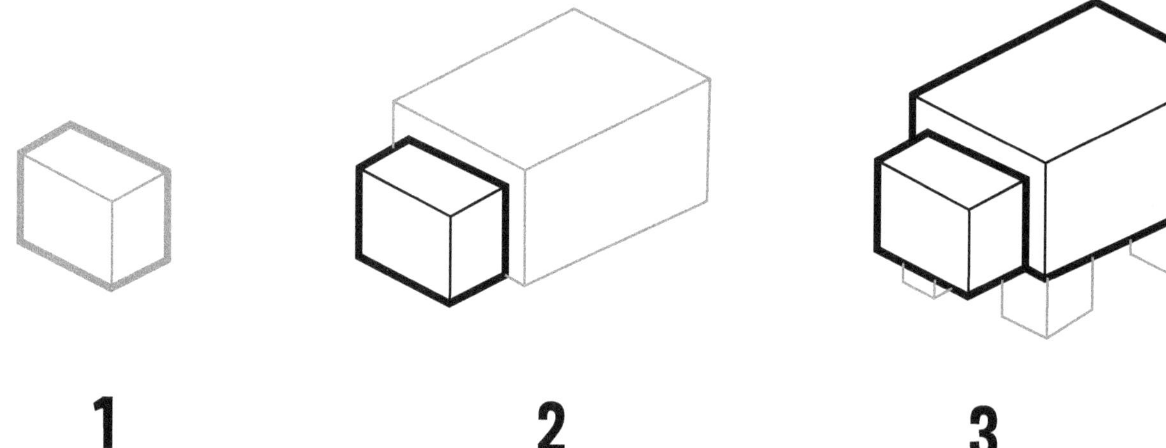

1

2

3

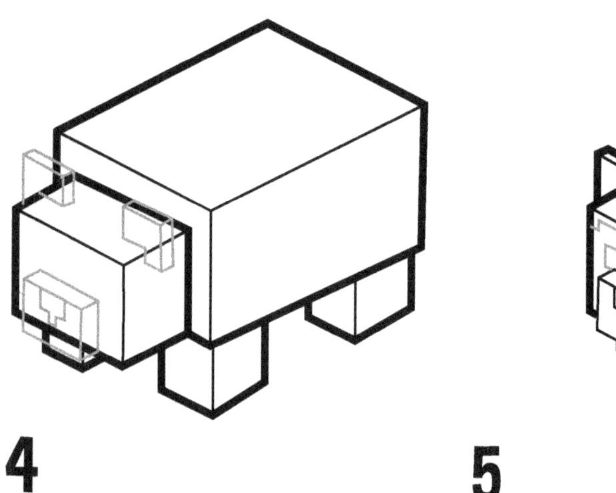

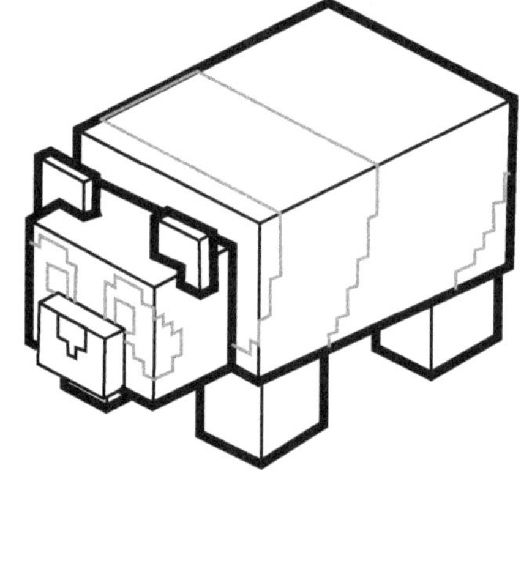

4

5

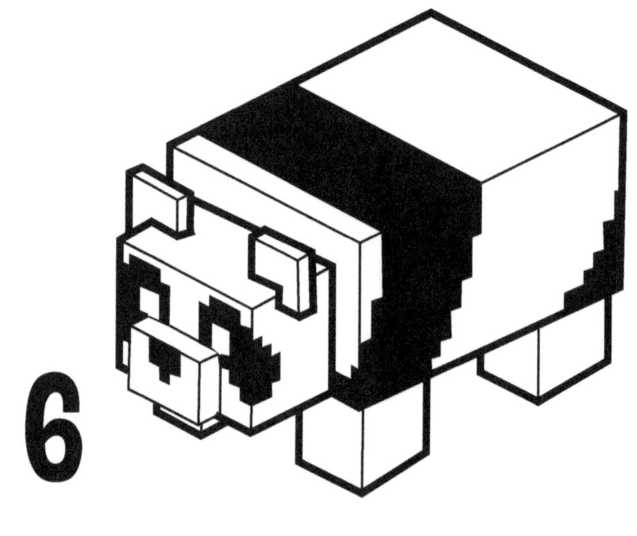

6

Now, it's your turn

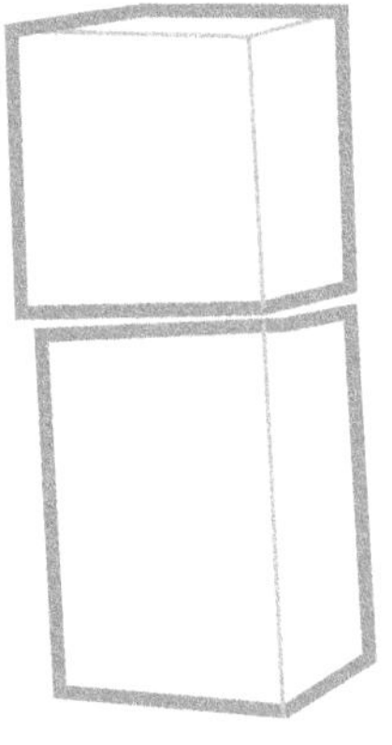

1

2

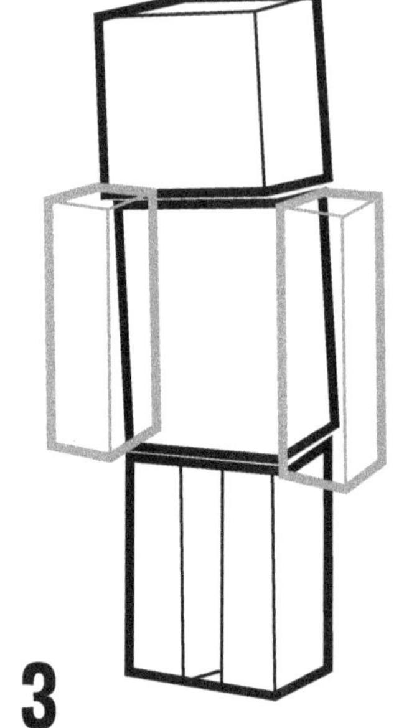

3

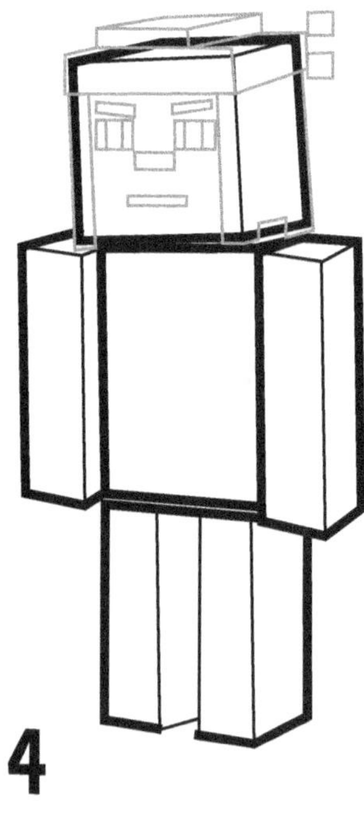

4

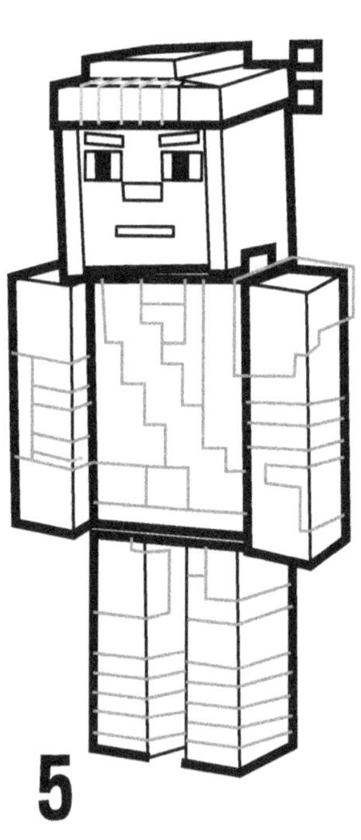

5

6

Now, it's your turn

How to draw: PIG

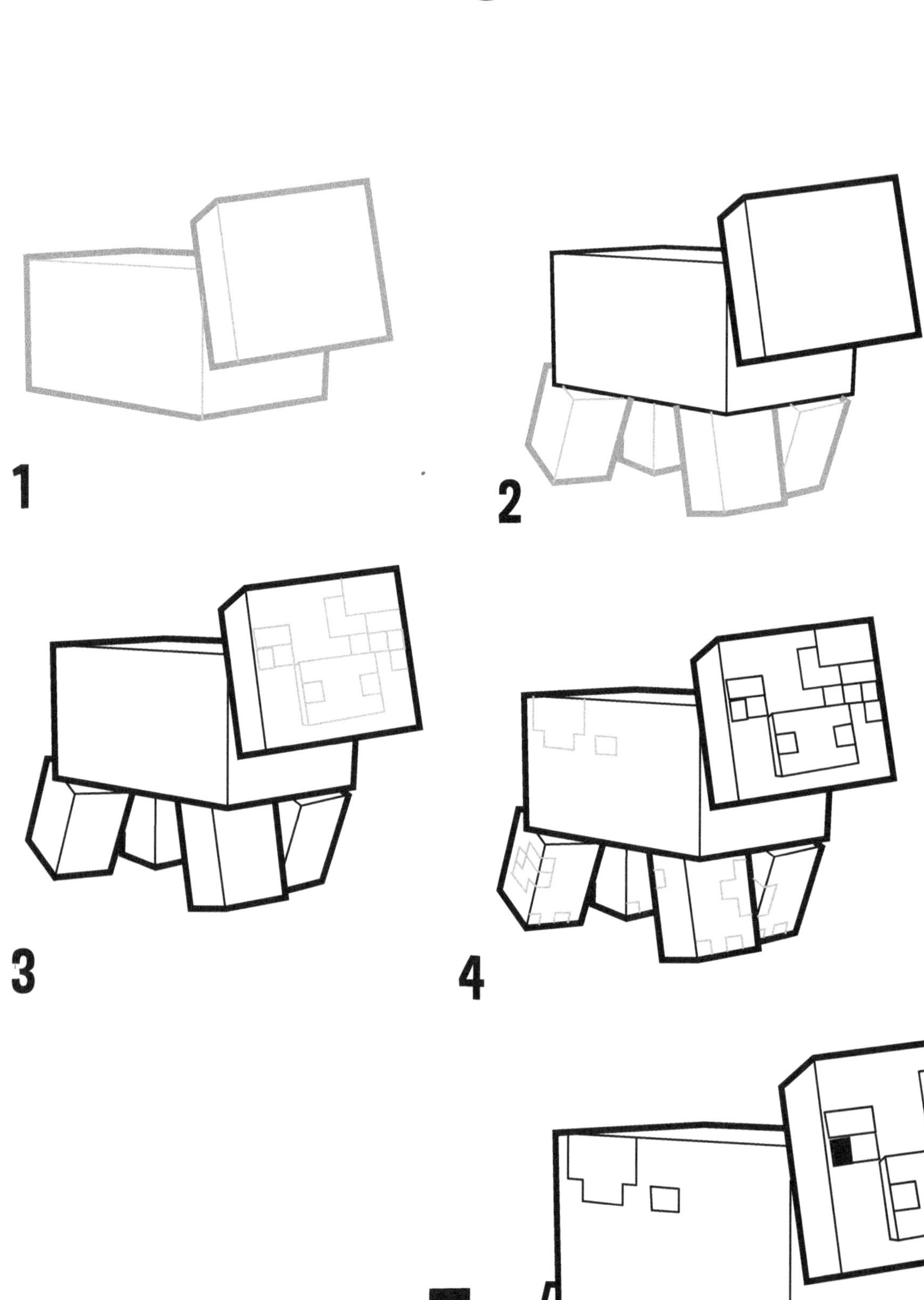

1

2

3

4

5

Now, it's your turn

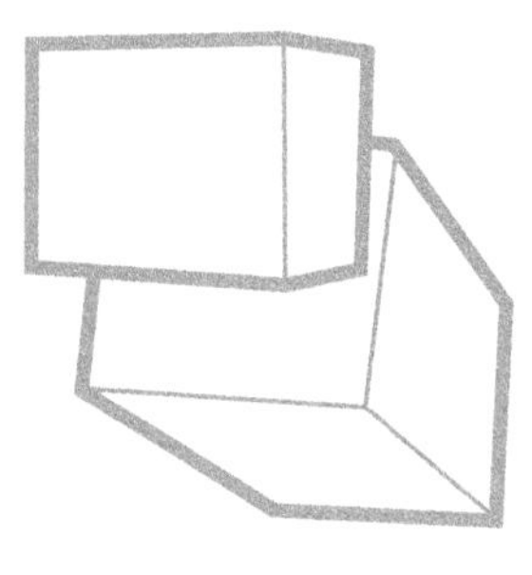

1

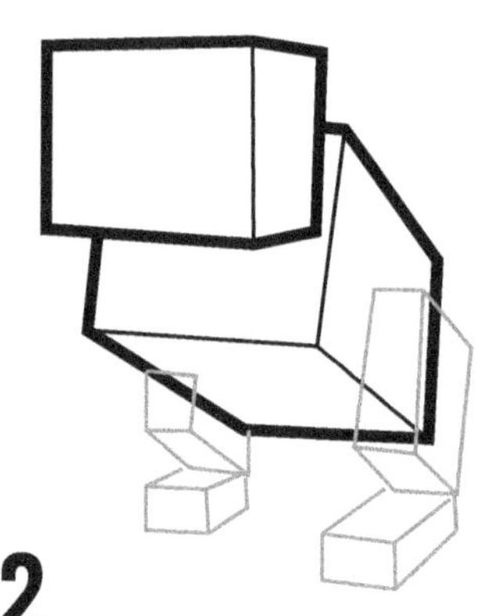

2

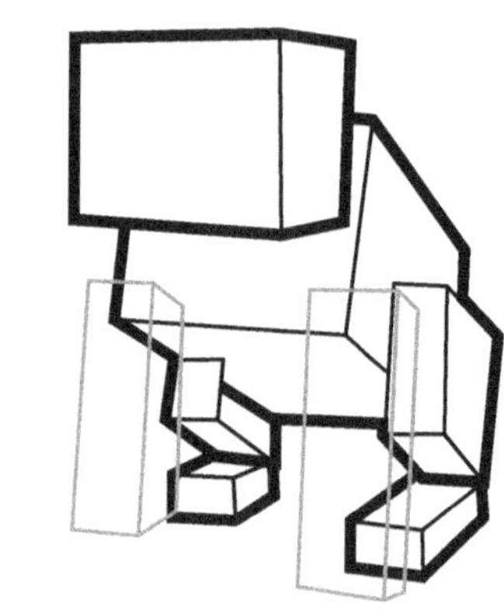

3

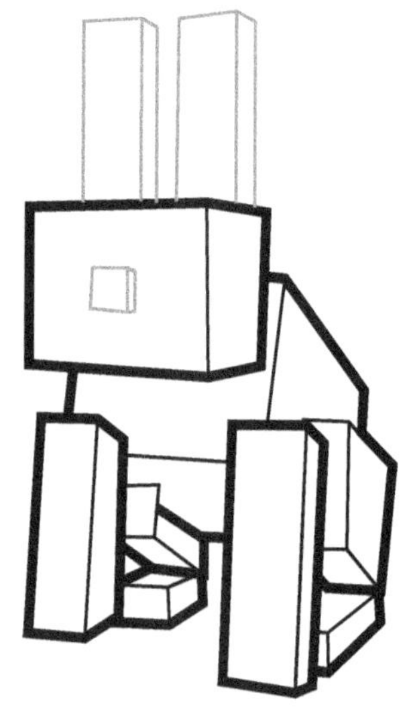

4

5

6

Now, it's your turn

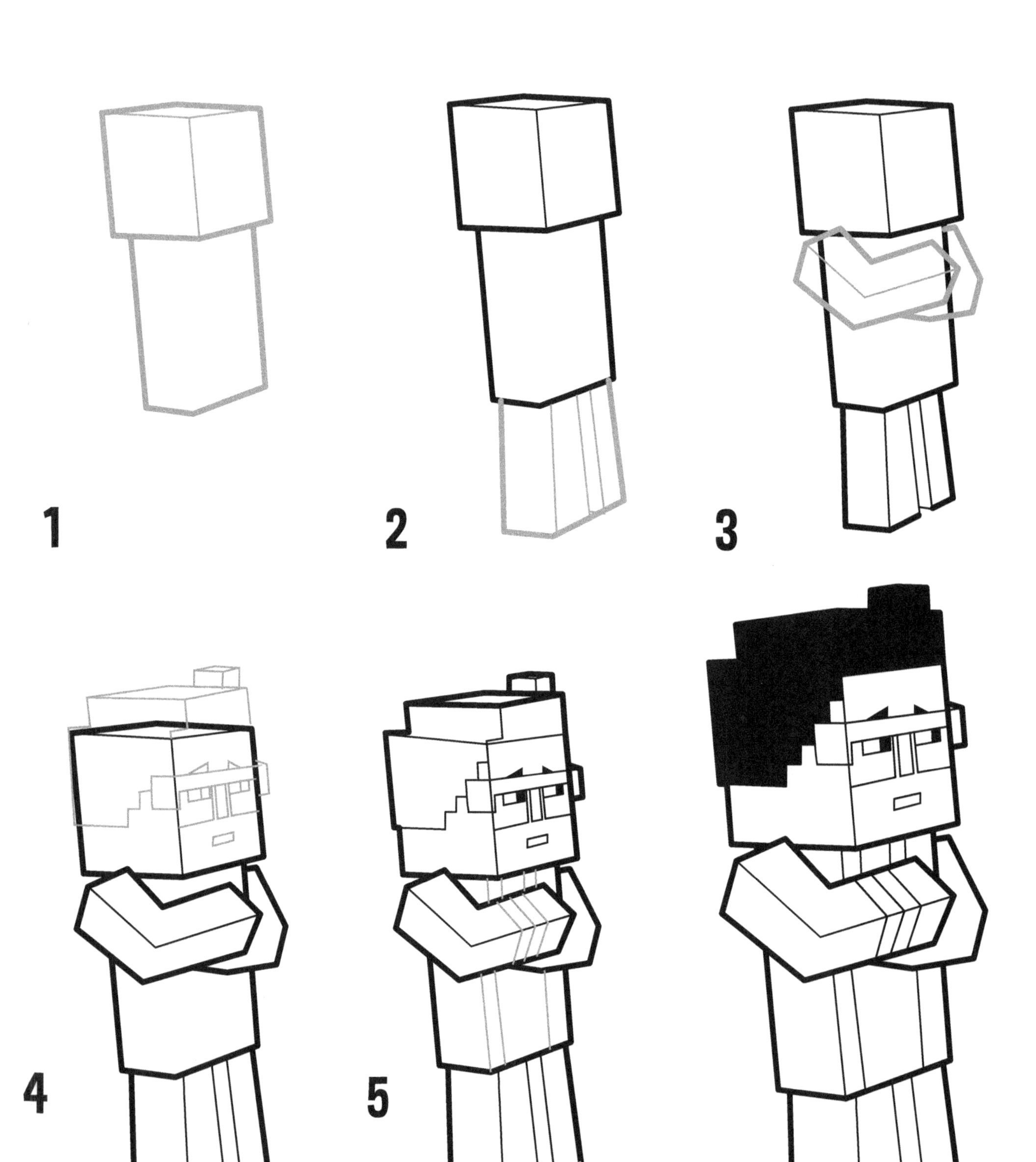

1
2
3
4
5
6

Now, it's your turn

How to draw: Redstone Monster

1

2

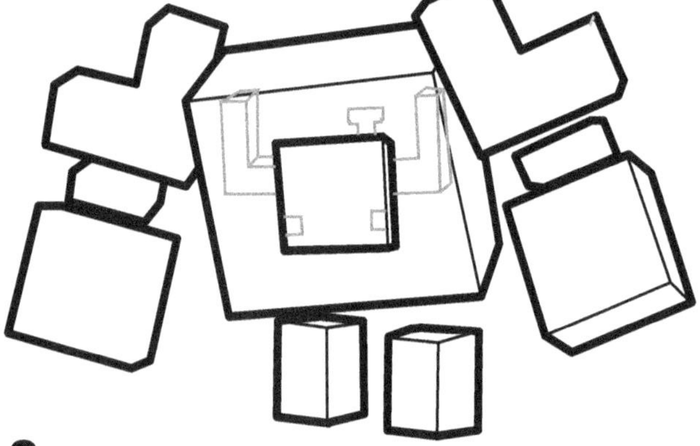

3

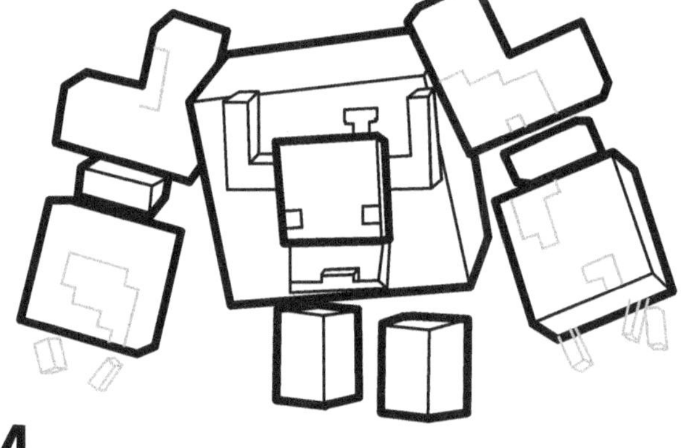

4

5

Now, it's your turn

How to draw: Royal Guard

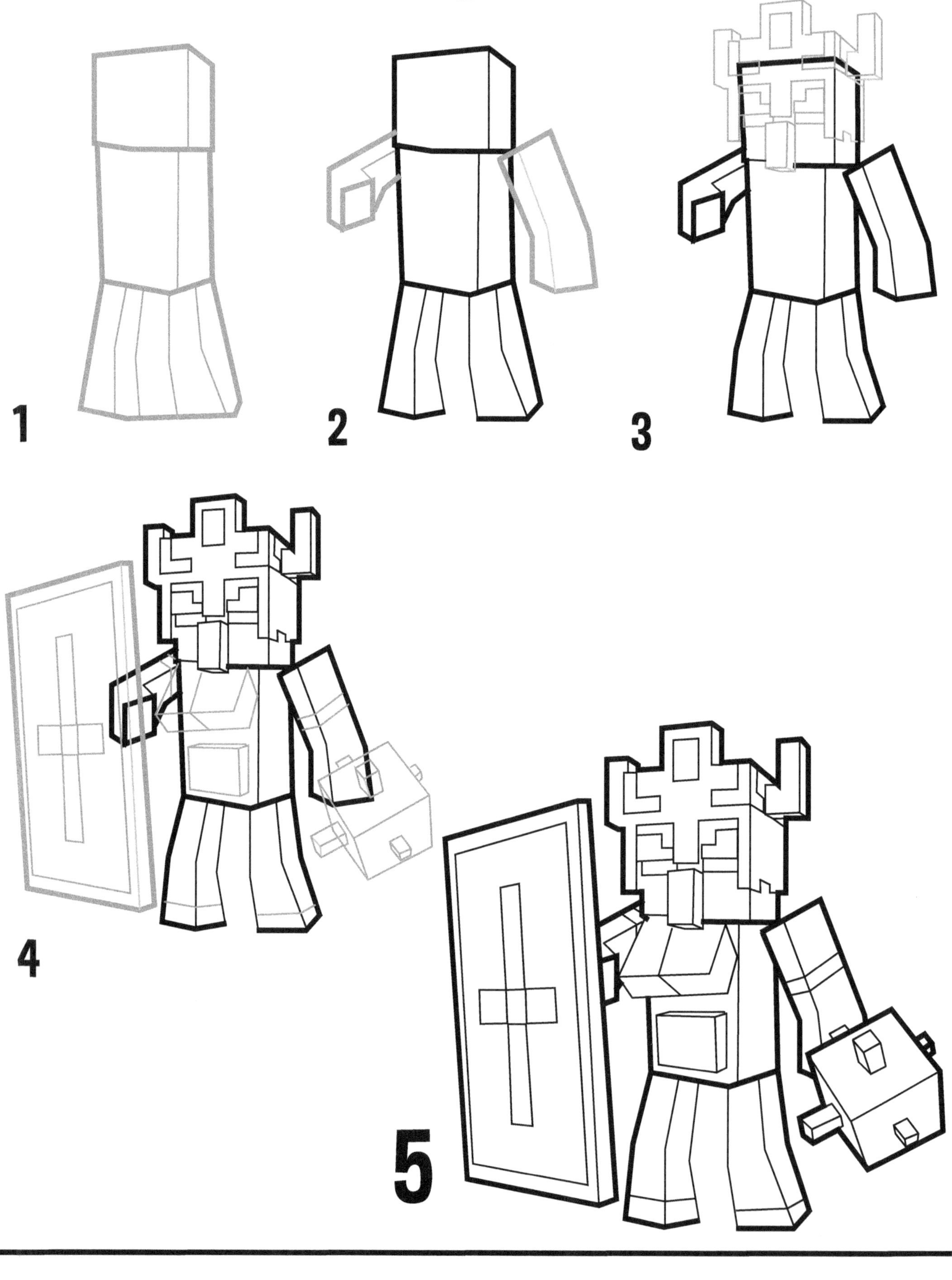

1

2

3

4

5

Now, it's your turn

How to draw: Snowman

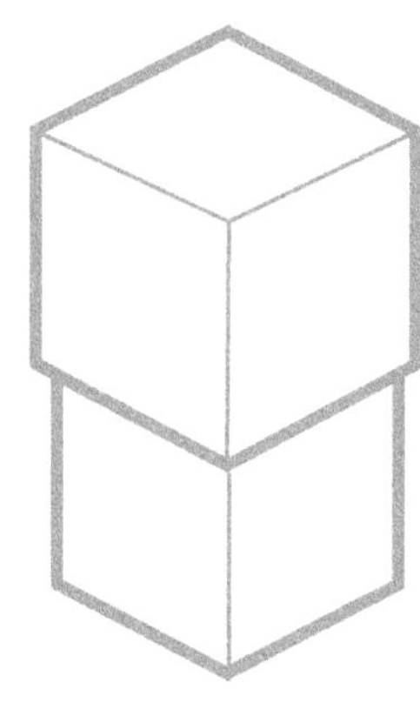

1

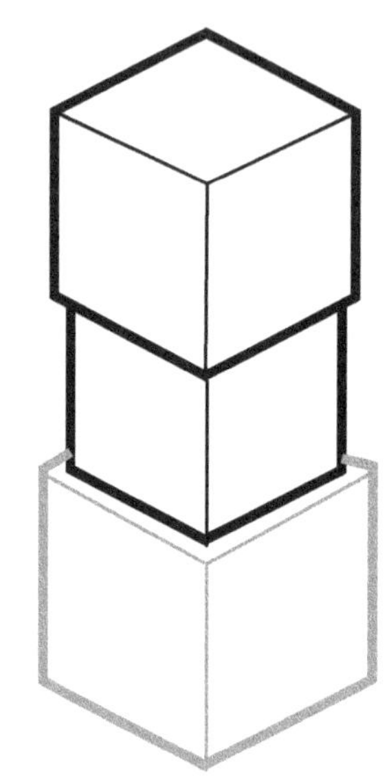

2

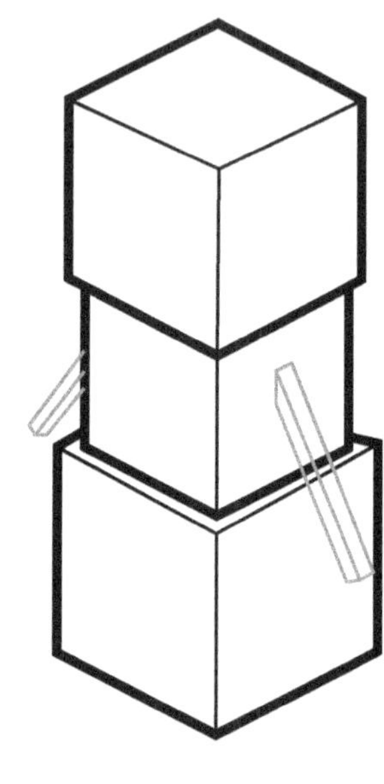

3

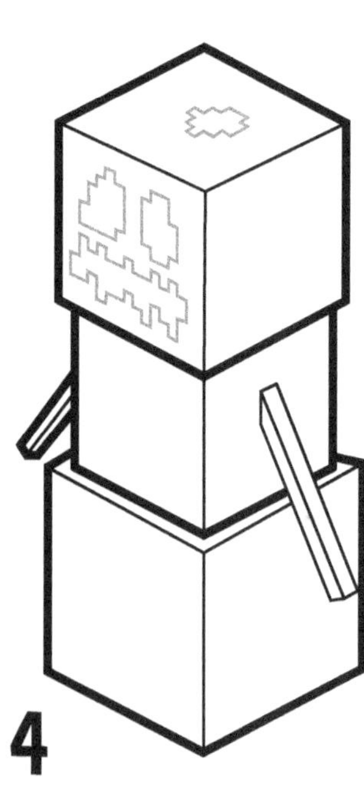

4

5

6

Now, it's your turn

How to draw: Soren

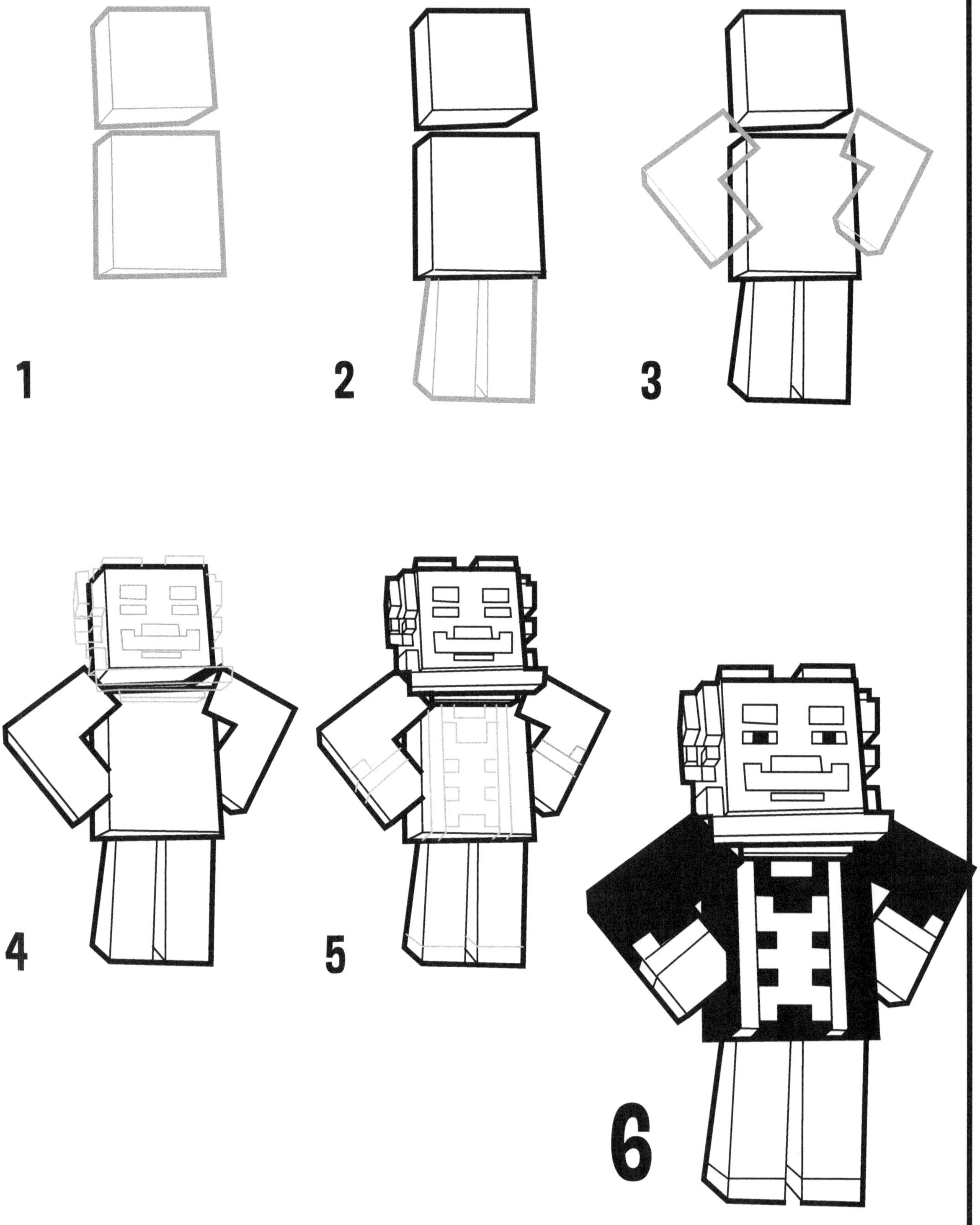

1

2

3

4

5

6

Now, it's your turn

Soul Healer

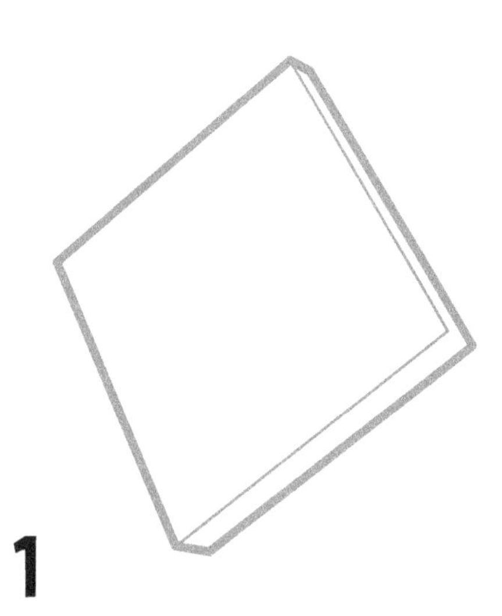

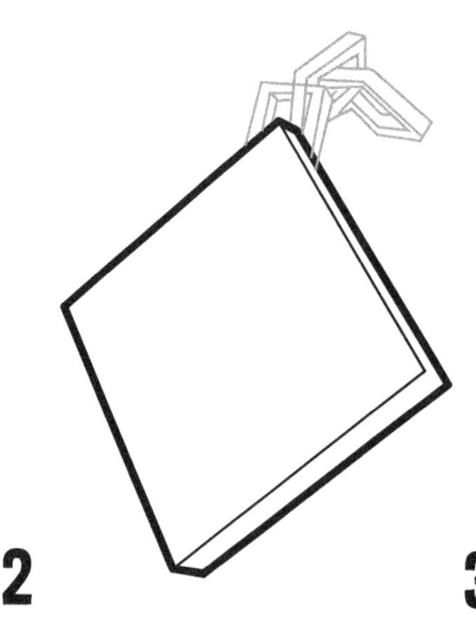

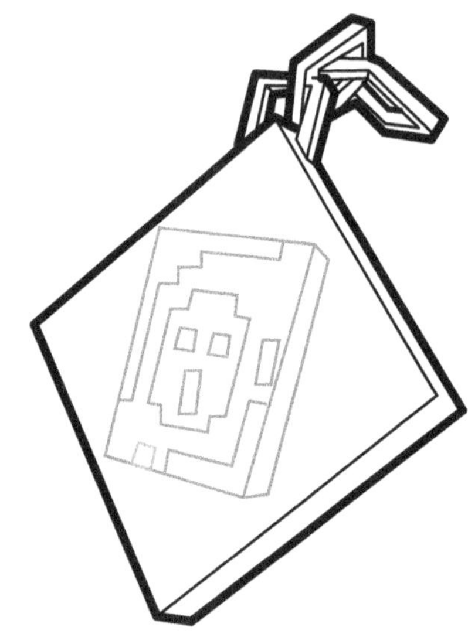

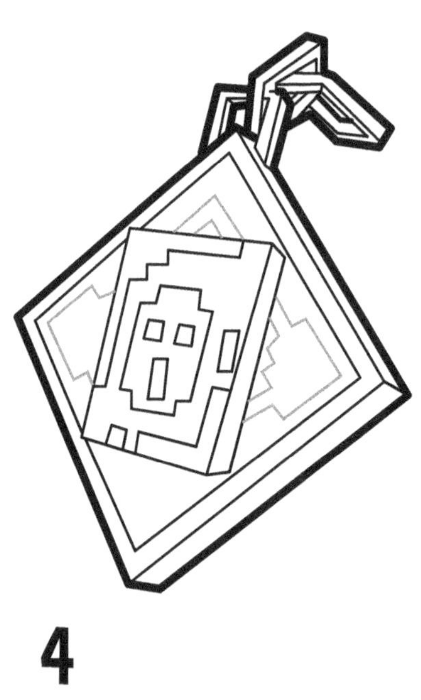

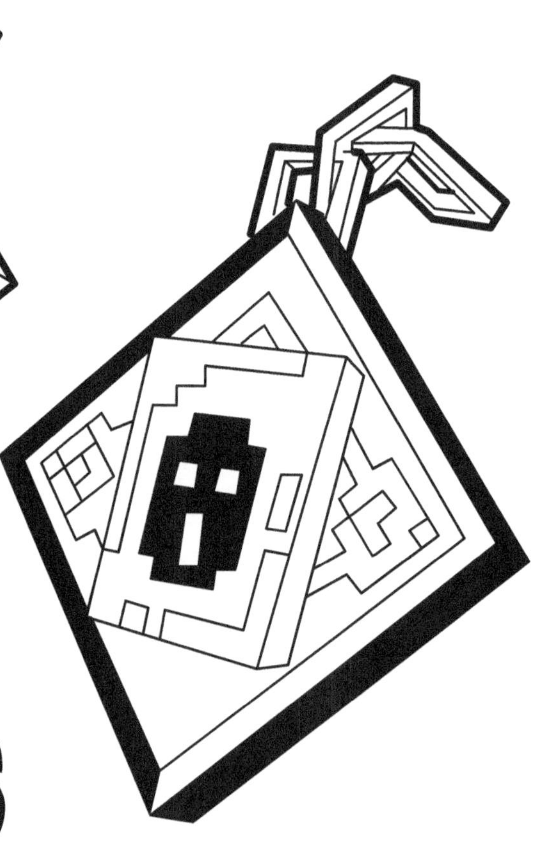

Now, it's your turn

Soul Lantern

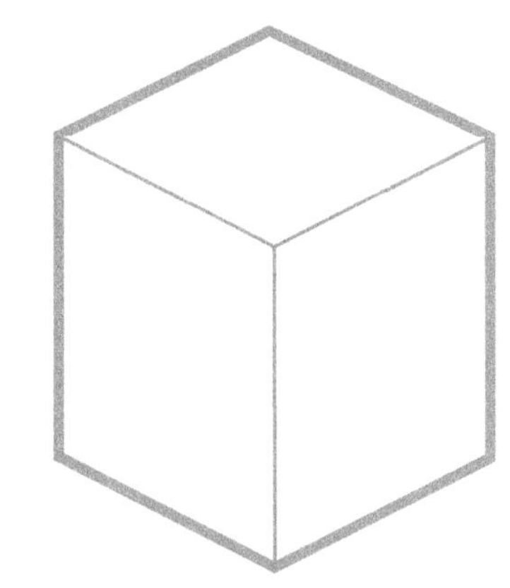

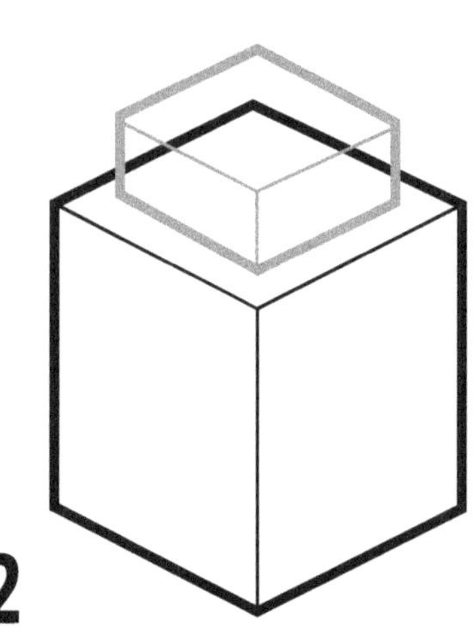

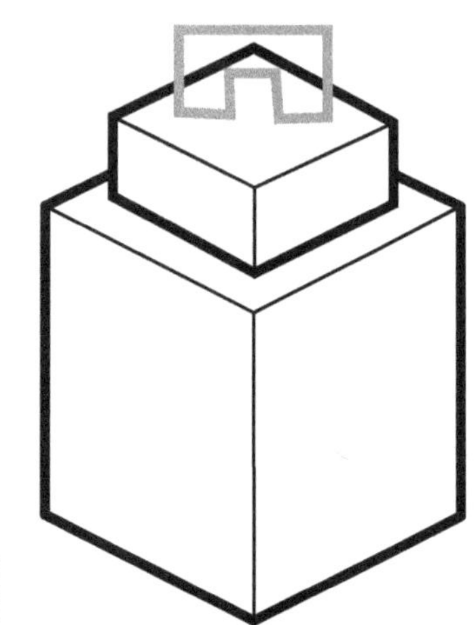

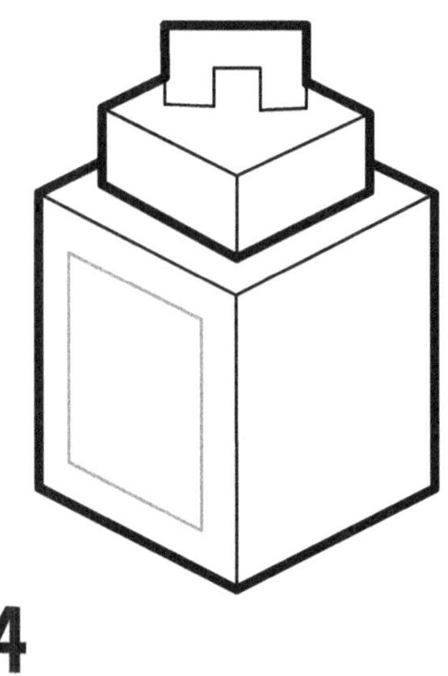

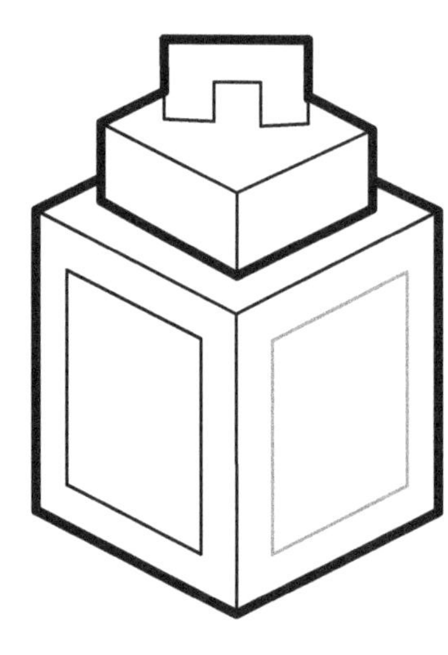

Now, it's your turn

How to draw: Soul Scythe

1

2

3

4

Now, it's your turn

How to draw:
Spider Armor

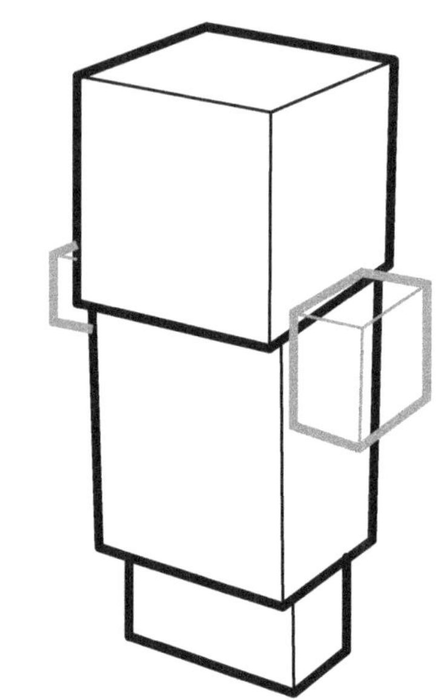

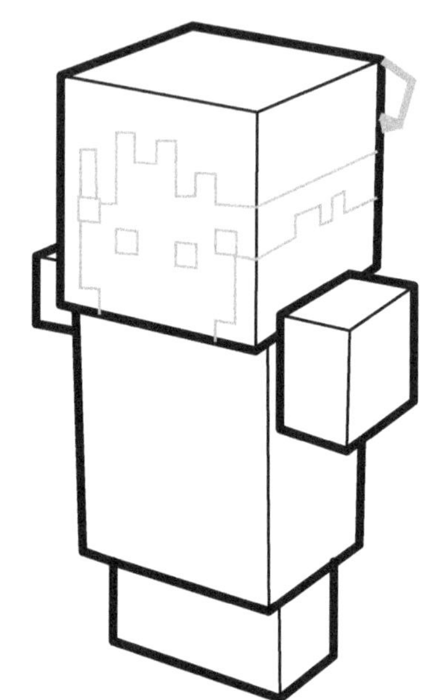

1
2
3
4
5

Now, it's your turn

How to draw: **Sword**

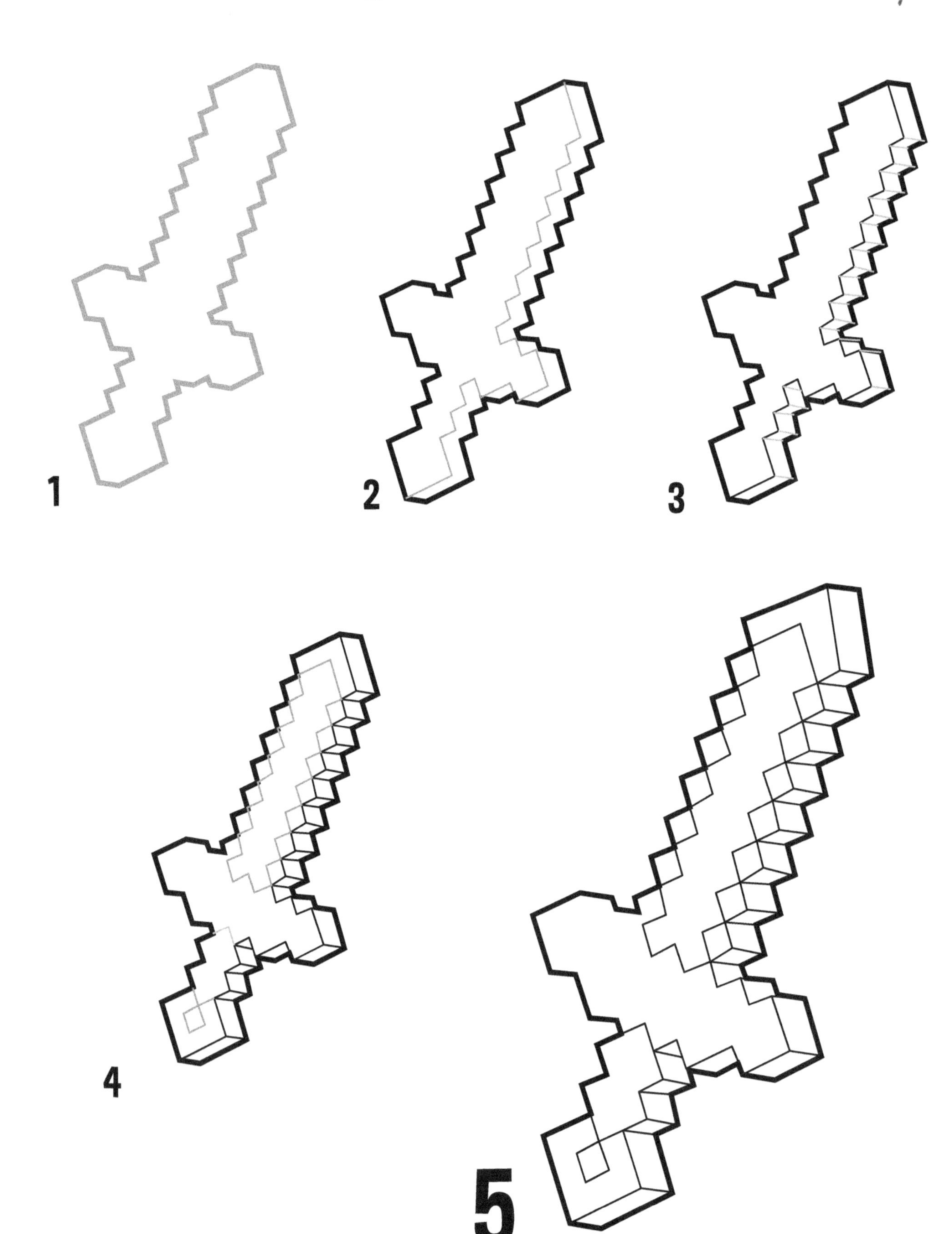

Now, it's your turn

How to draw: Totem of Shielding

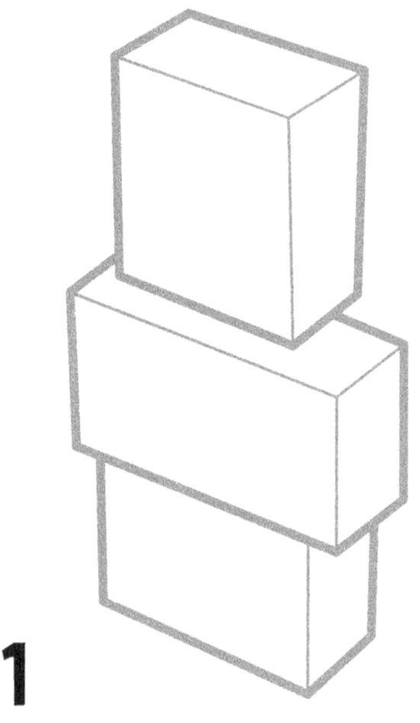

1

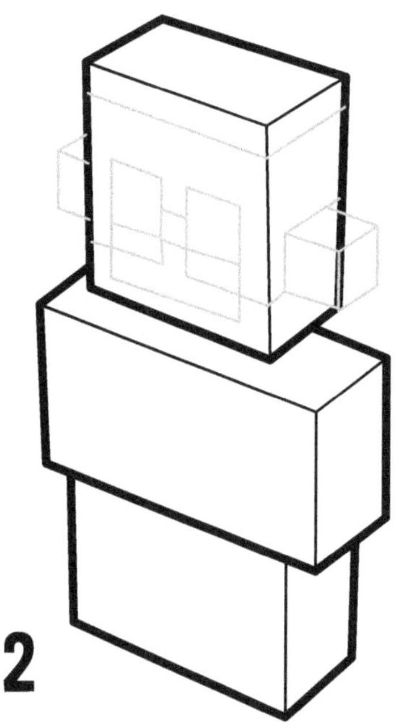

2

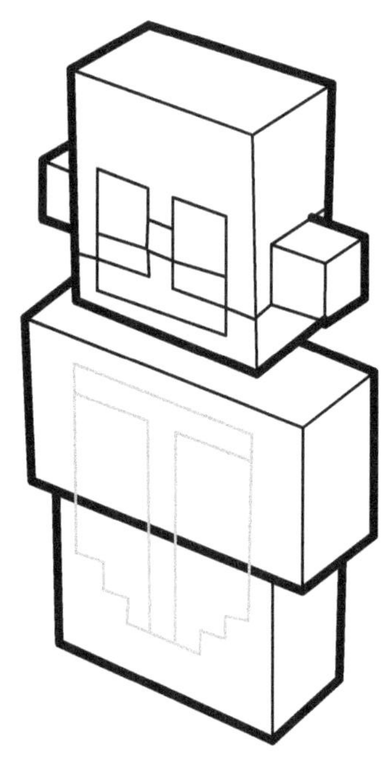

3

4

Now, it's your turn

How to draw: Trident
1
2
3

Now, it's your turn

How to draw: Turtle

1

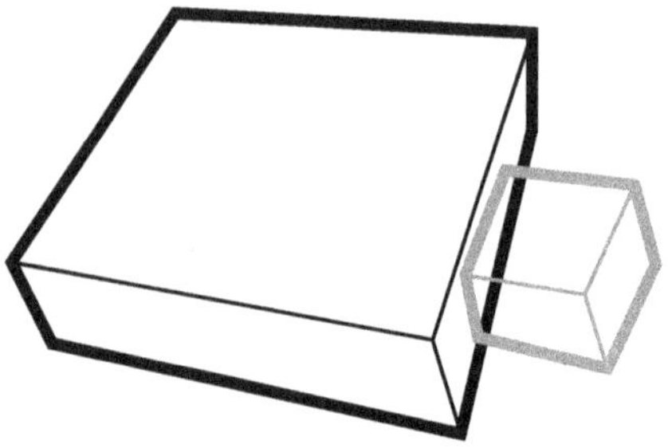

2

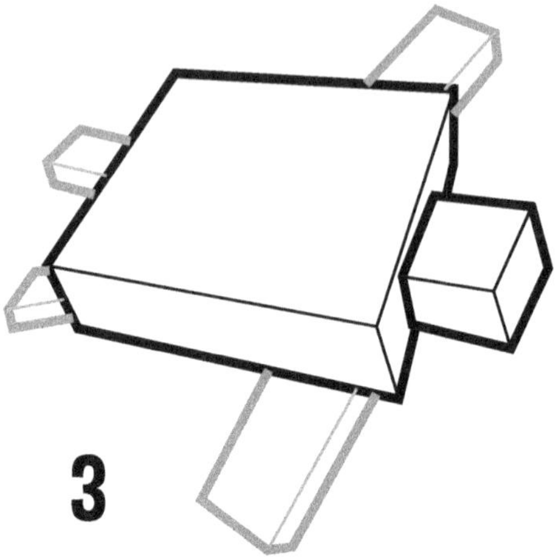

3

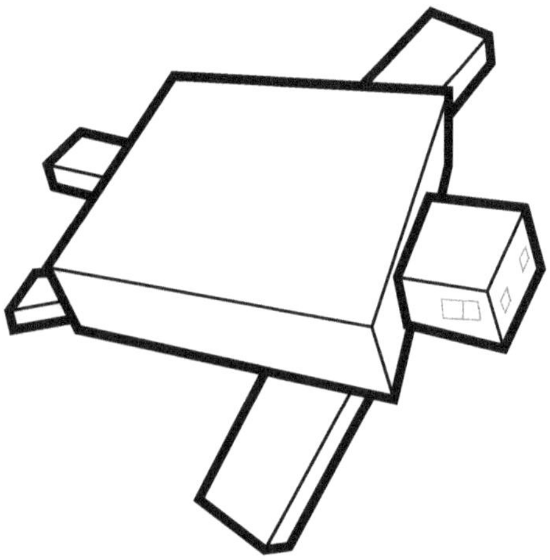

4

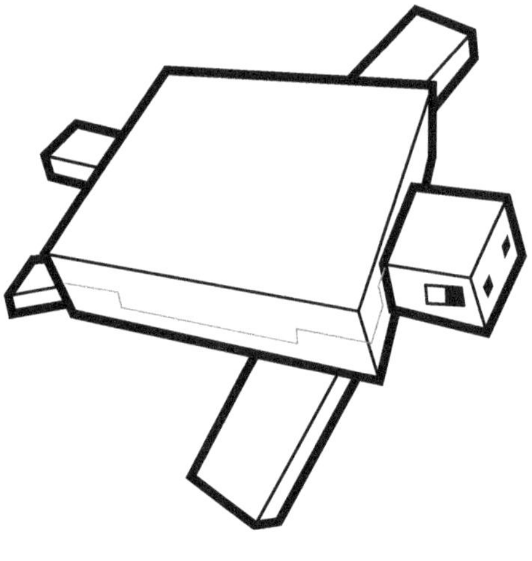

5

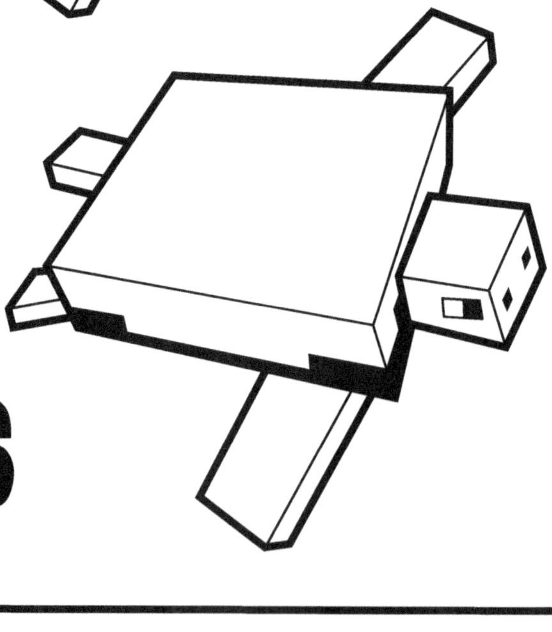

6

Now, it's your turn

How to draw: Vindicator

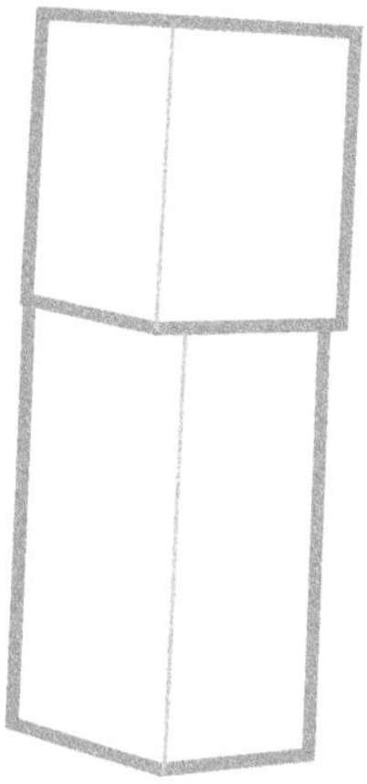

1

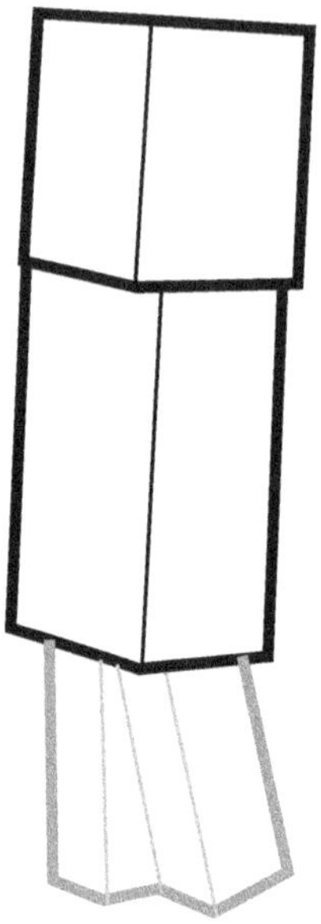

2

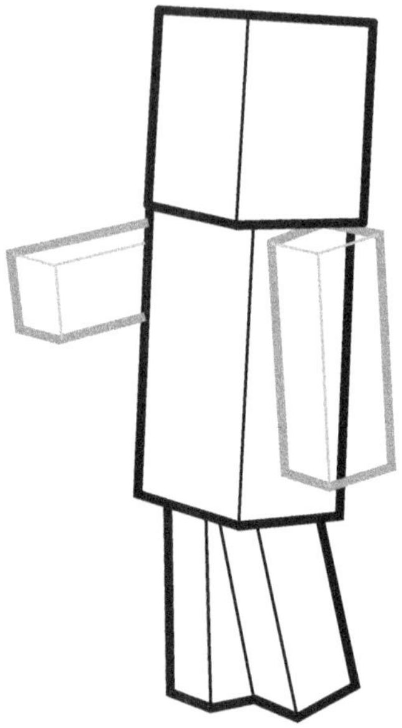

3

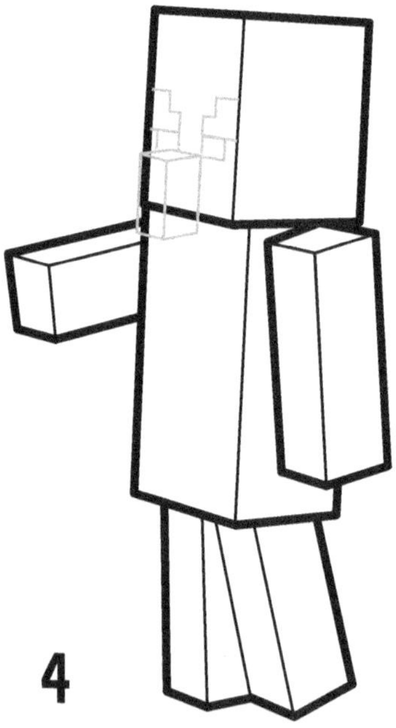

4

5

6

Now, it's your turn

How to draw: **Wolf**

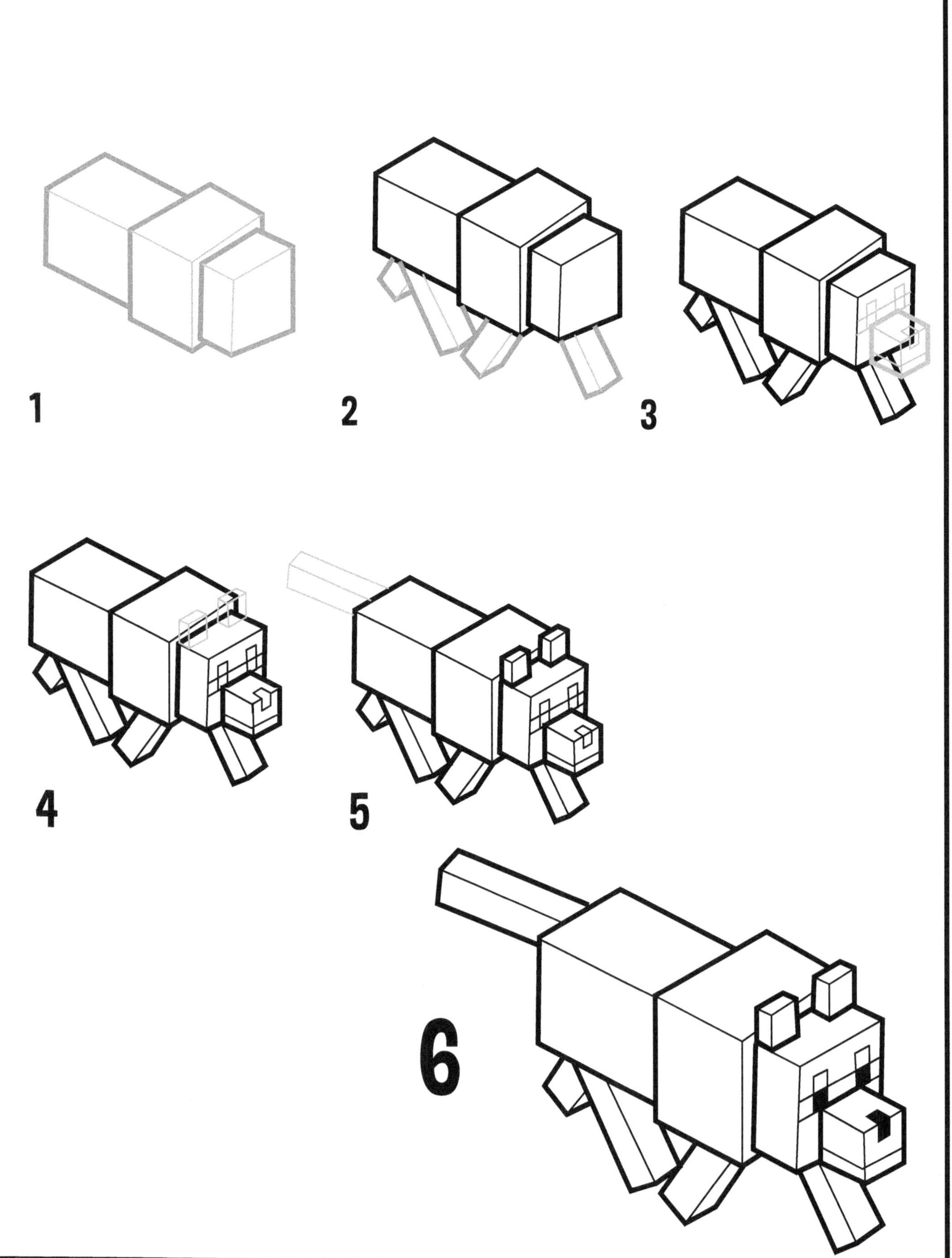

1

2

3

4

5

6

Now, it's your turn

How to draw: Wraith

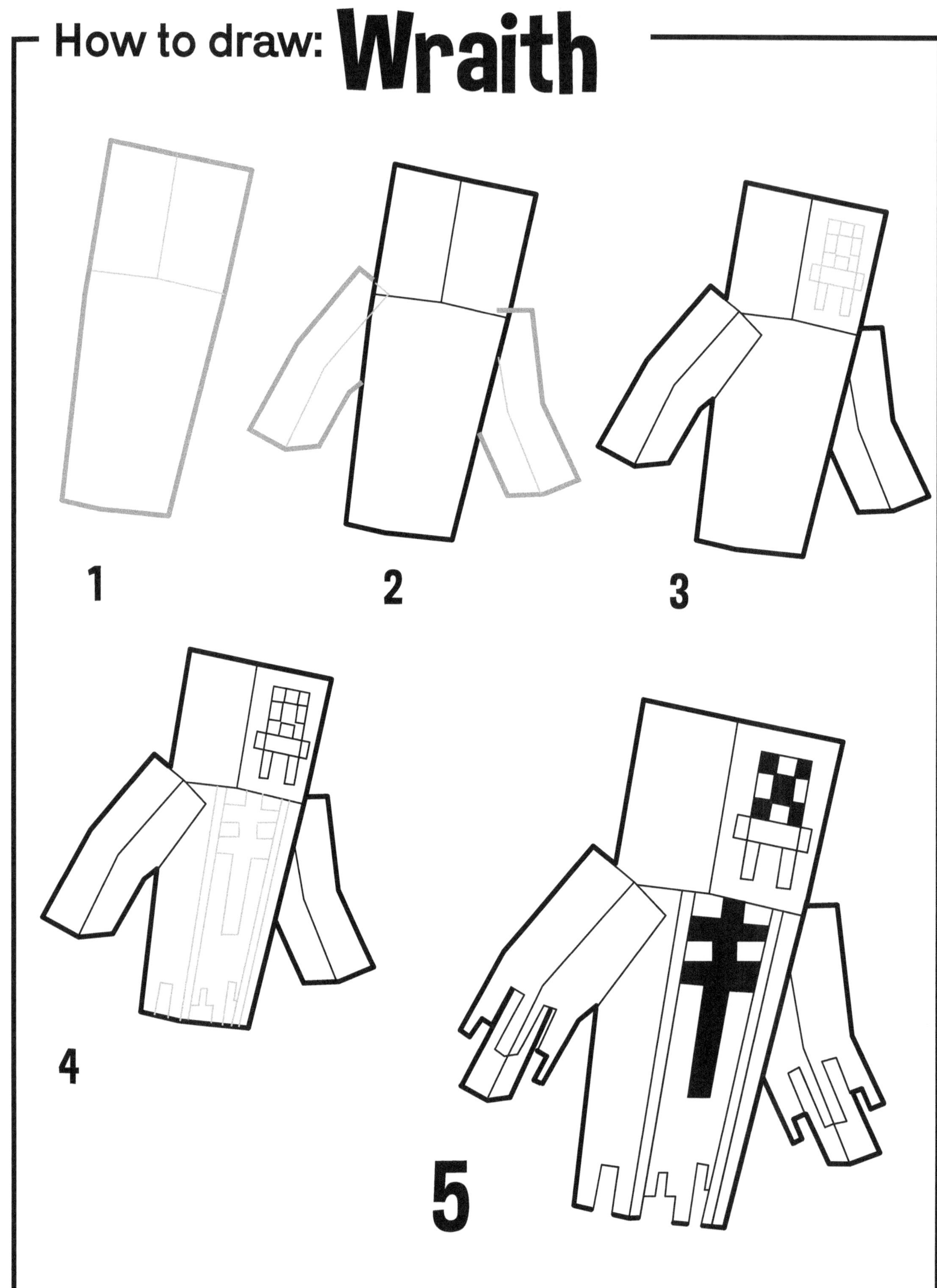

Now, it's your turn

How to draw: **Wretched Wraith**

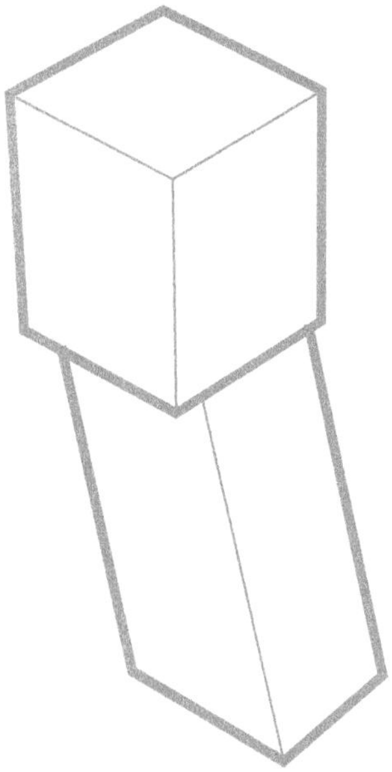

1

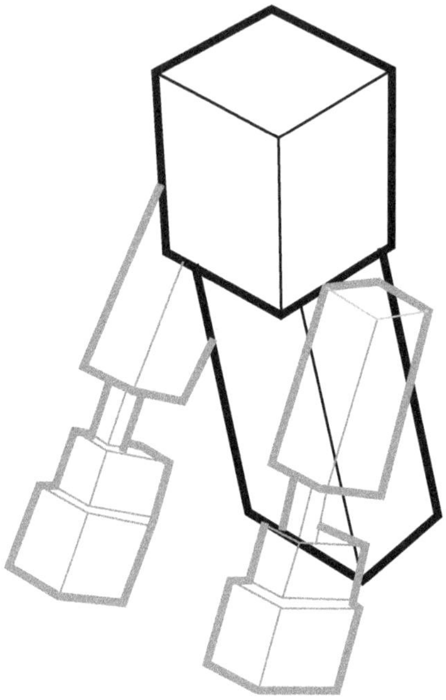

2

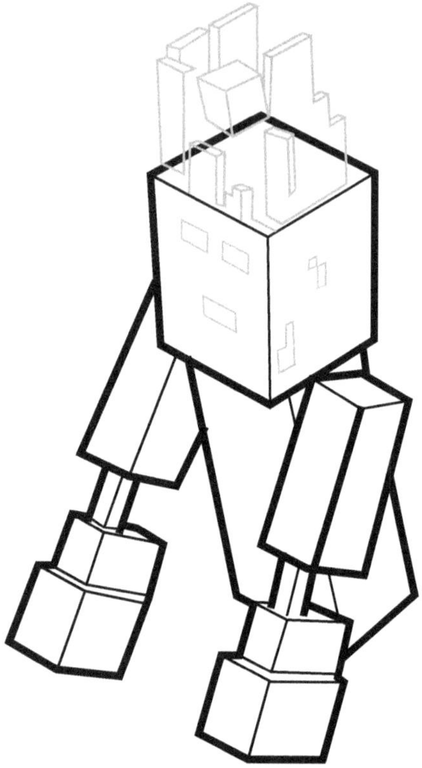

3

4

5

Now, it's your turn

DOWNLOAD 50
FREE COLORING PAGES

Visit our website or message to us!

WWW.CUBEHUNTER.NET